G000253108

The Illustrated History of
Derby's Suburbs

The Illustrated History of
Derby's Suburbs

by Maxwell Craven

The Breedon Books
Publishing Company
Derby

First published in Great Britain by
The Breedon Books Publishing Company Limited,
Breedon House, 44 Friar Gate, Derby, DE1 1DA.
1996

© Maxwell Craven 1996

All Rights Reserved. No part of this publication may be
reproduced, stored in a retrieval system, or transmitted in any
form, or by any means, electronic, mechanical, photocopying,
recording or otherwise without the prior permission in writing
of the Copyright holders, nor be otherwise circulated in any
form or binding or cover other than in which it is published
and without a similar condition being imposed on the
subsequent publisher.

ISBN 1 85983 031 5

Printed and bound by Butler & Tanner Ltd., Selwood Printing
Works, Caxton Road, Frome, Somerset.

Colour separations by Colour Services, Wigston, Leicester.

Contents

Acknowledgements

THE acquisition of expertise over a protracted period of time involves interaction with a great many people and groups from nearly all of whom (or which) I am proud to say that I have learned much. It would also be impossible to catalogue them all, but I stand in the debt of them all.

My long-suffering publisher, Mr Rippon and his colleagues also deserve my thanks. I am grateful that they encourage me to undertake further projects; I earnestly hope that the willingness of my readers to buy the resultant books helps to keep Breedon Books a viable entity! I am also extremely grateful to the elegantly unflappable Mrs Zoe Ware who typed the MS, a lady who can read my writing and still appear cheerful at the end of it!

Amongst those whom I wish to acknowledge personally are – in alphabetical order – the late Guy Brighouse, the late Ken Brown, the late Cliff Burton, the late Maj. J.W.Chandos-Pole, Roy Christian MBE, Norma Consterdine, Leslie Cox, James Darwin, the late Patrick Drury-Lowe, Kevin Ellis, Sir Henry Every, Bt., Don Farnsworth, Ian Griffiths, D. & J.Harpur Esqrs., Mark Higginson, Robert Innes-Smith, Viv Irish and her ever-delightful colleagues on *Derbyshire Life*, the late Dorothy Jeffrey, Mrs E.Kitchin, Josef Lachowicz, Richard Langley, Derek Limer, the staff of Derby Local Studies Library (without whom nothing would ever get written by a local historian), Roger Pegg, Jim Regan, Laurence Sanders, Michael Shaw, Jane Steer, Helen Young and John Young. The front cover view of the fire at the former Burrows and Sturgess factory on Slack Lane, Derby was photographed by Pip Southall.

Whilst I hesitate to claim this list as exhaustive, I would like to take this opportunity to apologise to anyone I have inadvertently omitted. it is also, in re-reading it, so sad that so many who have been such help and encouragement have died in the last year or so. I shall miss them dearly.

Finally, and as so often before, I must thank my wife Carole for her forbearance, proofreading, encouragement, willingness to drive to obscure suburban streets, and in suffering all the domestic infelicities which arise from being married to a writer. Her constant cheerfulness and willingness to help have been my inspiration.

Maxwell Craven
Derby
May 1996

Introduction

IDEALLY, the suburbs of Derby deserve their own detailed Illustrated History, perhaps uniform with the similarly named volume on Derby which I had the privilege of writing in 1988. That way, each suburb could be chronicled by its own historians and the whole given uniformity by an editor.

This volume seeks only to be an appetiser. It consists of illustrations of suburban scenes with captions, each suburb being introduced, not by a serious attempt to provide a history – space does not permit – but by a highly-personalised thumbnail sketch which looks to explain the relevant settlements, origins and integration (or, in some cases, de-integration) with Central Derby.

Because these thumbnail sketches are of necessity selective and brief, I have eschewed compiling a formal bibliography but have appended a few suggestions at the end of each entry suggesting further reading. For those with a copy of my *Illustrated History of Derby*, the reference therein to fuller remarks about each suburb is noted, similarly with the suburban seats, from my *Derby Town House* (1987) and *The Derbyshire Country House* (1984 & 1991). Sir Nicholas Pevsner's *The Buildings of England* series on Derbyshire (Revised edition, 1978) is helpful for other notable buildings, as are the City Council's *Statutory List for Derby* and the Derby *Local List*. On churches, Dr J.C.Cox's monumental *Notes on the Churches of Derbyshire* (4 vols, Derby & London 1877-1879) is very helpful. It will be noted that some suburbs have yet to find an analyst, and others need a contemporary one. Local groups could look to the Normanton Local History Group's elegant volume on that suburb (also published by Breedon Books two years ago) as an exemplar, although the need for a good index cannot be over-emphasised.

The town of Derby had a double origin, of course. The Romans founded a fort of unknown extent on the high ground to the west of the Derwent about a mile north of the city centre. This was replaced, we believe, in the later first century, by what became a largely civilian settlement on the low-lying ground to the east of the Derwent and controlling its lowest crossing point. By the early fifth century this town – *Derventio* – had declined, and at an unknown date following the conversion of Mercia to Christianity (*c*.660) a century and a half later, a minister church was built south of the abandoned Roman settlement, on a ridge bounded on the east by the Derwent and on the south and west by the Markeaton Brook.

This church, with its six missionary priests – canons – later became St Alkmund's and was the focus of a small community of priests and those who saw to their needs which gathered in the precinct of the minister beside the prehistoric north-south trackway linking north Leicestershire with the upper Derwent Valley via the Trent, which it crossed on a causeway and ford at Swarkestone, later Swarkestone Bridge.

The minister of St Alkmund – so named after the Northumbrian martyr-prince whose remains were re-interred within it for safety from the Danes early in the ninth century – lay within an extensive tract of countryside which may have centred on the Saxon monastery of Breedon or the royal centre of Repton. This area was called Northworthy, a name subsequently and, we believe, erroneously attributed to Derby itself by a later chronicler. The tract, lying largely north of the Trent and between the Rivers Derwent and Dove belonged as a unity to the Mercian Royal House, and was captured intact by the Vikings in 874, when they deposed the Mercian King and sacked St Alkmund's and its small community. Scattered across Northworthy were a number of settlements – then dispersed rather than nucleated ones – which were the forerunners of the villages which later did become nucleated and many of which subsequently became the suburbs absorbed by Derby's modern expansion.

The Vikings probably settled the site of *Derventio*, undoubtedly re-fortified the 25ft high Roman defensive walls and re-named it *Deoraby* – Derby. They also settled Normanton (qv.), Ingleby near Repton and elsewhere.

Their power was broken in 917 by Queen Aethelflaeda of Mercia who defeated the Norse at *Derventio*, and by 941 the Saxon Kingdom of All England was re-established. A decade or two prior to that date, a new town was founded, centring on the restored minister of St Alkmund, and bearing the transferred name Derby. The Norse settlement within *Derventio* survived as Little Chester, and it, with Little Eaton and Quarndon, were given to the new *burgh* as endowments of the new Free Chapel Royal of All Saints', thus constituting Derby's earliest suburbs.

Between Derby's foundation and the Norman Conquest in 1066, the town had flourished and absorbed one or two of the settlements of greater Northworthy, which itself had effectively ceased to exist through having been broken up by Aethelflaeda or her successors to reward with land those followers who had helped with the ejection of the Danes. Some of the absorbed settlements – also proto-suburbs – were Wardwick (qv), Litchurch, probably Morledge and possibly Doglow and Haye. Further, Saxon or Norse grandees like the Algar Earl of Mercia and Toki, who held estates in the countryside, founded urban churches – at least six by 1066 – linked to their country properties on which were chapels-of-ease of the urban foundations, sometimes sharing the same dedication. Hence St Michael's Alvaston was part of the Derby parish of St Michael – they were both part of the same feudal holding, or fee – and Boulton, Normanton, Osmaston and Codington pertained to St Peters, and so on. Thus, although these villages remained country settlements, they had ancient links with Derby which gave them a certain suburban status which was reinforced after 1901 by direct absorption into the body politic of the County Borough of Derby.

Therefore the suburbs described and pictured in this book are many and varied in nature ranging from the medieval settlements described to relatively new suburbs. Some are small localities, some large rather amorphous sprawling villages absorbed by the expansion of the city's boundaries. I have tried to include all suburbs, including ancient ones, to make the record complete, but there are anomalies. I have frequently stated that, prior to Derby's foundation, after 917, a village called Wardwick with its proprietorial chapel dedicated to St Werburgh existed. This was absorbed so early, and is so central, that I have treated it as part of the city centre and omitted it. Some localities, like Rose Hill, are difficult to disinter as entities (it was entirely surrounded by Litchurch) that I have lumped them in with larger units. The same goes for Pear Tree, which has got but one view included here, although several Litchurch, New Normanton and Normanton views take in other portions of it.

Other suburbs, like Quarndon and Little Eaton, were once attached to Derby but are no longer; they are, however, included. Ockbrook and Stenson have never been part of Derby, but have been included entirely through author's whim. Part of Stenson (parish of Twyford) has, however, been invaded by the extra-urban part of the Sinfin housing development. Another contiguous village, Breadsall, has long had its territory split between Derby and the neighbouring authority – roughly along the lines of the medieval split between its Nether Hall and Upper Hall manors. I have taken the liberty of including the whole parish, all entirely of my own volition: there is no corporate hidden agenda!

Finally, one important suburb has been entirely omitted: Oakwood, created over the past 15 years in portions of Breadsall and Chaddesden. A second primary aim of this volume is to enable the publication of yet more of the Museum's vast holdings of photographs of the city (totalling 13,130 prints as I write, not to mention some 2,000 slides). Whilst it is to be hoped that posterity will be grateful for the efforts that have been made to amass them over the past 20 or so years, present generations have little chance of enjoying them on display, as no gallery yet exists to chart the history of the city. Thus, in collecting more of them together in the present work, it is to be hoped they will bring pleasure to the nostalgic, enlightenment to the local historian and amazement to the general reader. Thus it is that these views attempt to trace not only the flavour of individual suburbs and communities, but also their development. The cut-off point is about 25 years ago, which means that the vast preponderance of views in this book were taken between 1901 and 1971. Thus Oakwood did not even exist at the cut-off date – except as an attractive tract of countryside containing vestiges of man's settlement from Roman to medieval times! Therefore, it will be to a future chronicler of the city that the duty of recording Oakwood, and now Heatherton will fall.

To some extent the choice of photographs was dictated by what was available. Another factor was the need to avoid re-publishing views which would already be familiar. In fact, I estimate that over 80% of the views in this book are previously unpublished (except as postcards at the turn of the century, in some cases). Thus obvious landmarks in main villages or suburbs, like famous buildings, churches or manors will have been left out in favour of agreeable if less famous buildings, chapels or villas, and a great emphasis has been laid on residential streets. The final choice, however, was the publisher's. These streets are not only the element which so rapidly devoured the pristine countryside, they are also where some 90% of the city's population now live, although in some cases, like

Little City and the West End, the houses have been cleared, and their inhabitants moved yet further out. Thus, this book panders to the localities of Derby, and of our locally-born or locally-based readers, this means that somewhere herein will be a place you know well.

As always with books of this kind, I have worked very hard to correctly identify and date the pictures, as well as produce accurate information in the introductory articles. This is not only vital for the reader, but for the usefulness of the photographs as part of the Museum's archive. A misidentified photograph is unlikely to help anyone. In most cases there has been little problem, but some prints have information written on their mounts which I have had to rely on entirely for identity.

In a few cases I felt that such information was suspect and have tried to be more accurate by touring the relevant neighbourhood, asking other experts or, thanks largely to Pam Carter, persuading the local paper to publish the view in question in order to encourage the readership to help me out. Inevitably there will still be the odd slip, I am sure, but I would ask the reader not only to take a tolerant view, but also to write to me with any amendments, so that at least future generations will have 100% accurate data available; then such information would be warmly welcomed. After all, as a non-native, your author's entire knowledge of Derby has been supplemented and brought alive through learning from people who know the city intimately, those who have specific memories or have made special studies of aspects of Derby life, past and present.

The captions, of course, are there to locate and date a scene. But also I have tried to use them to amplify my prefatory remarks about each suburb or locality. Thus, together, they may be taken as a useful contribution to the growing body of published knowledge about our amiable city. Where the Museum has a negative of a relevant photograph, a serial number has been printed. Should a reader wish to order a print from the museum it is valuable to quote the number.

It was intimated earlier that some localities were hard to tie down. Many suburbs of Derby have changed their boundaries over the years. Others are extremely hard to define on the ground. Thus, some readers may be horrified to find their personal area mentioned under a heading which wouldn't have occurred to them. If this causes ruffled feathers, then I must apologise in advance: if it causes a fuss when a reduction in Council Tax assessment is sought on the strength of your author's view of the boundaries of, say, Littleover, then I have to apologise, for such things are never going to carry that sort of weight!

Finally, if there is a scene in this book which shows an area fairly near to where you live or have lived, do not hesitate to contact the Museum's Antiquities Department, where the photographic collection is housed; for each view here, several others will also be on file. But do bear in mind that for 'inner city' or old suburbs, no one thought to photograph those grim streets, and few of the families living in them in the old days owned even a Box Brownie. Thus such views are very scarce.

Most 'inner city' views (as will be apparent from the pages which follow) were actually taken by planning and housing officers in the immediate post-war period. Frequently, therefore, the subject of their photographs will be well past their prime. Any new material which the Museum could copy, however, would be extremely welcome.

Finally, to the casual reader with no connection with Derby, I apologise: these pages will probably not excite you, for they represent a little bit of parochial self-indulgence on the part of the rest of us!

Population	Area (in acres)	Population						
		1801	1831	1841	1861	1881	1901	1931
Allenton		-	-	-	-	-	450*	450
Allestree	1057	350	501	507	557	586	589	1412
Alvaston	1534	-	-	493	504	2600	2485	8982
Boulton	791	-	-	171	-	-	2040	5056
Breadsall	2219	414	565	620	621	530	515	1441‡
Burnaston	988	-	-	143	-	171	219	196
Chaddesden	2089	502	469	472	433	611	567	1982
Chellaston	831	205	352	461	499	498	465	1292
Cottons	-	-	-	-	-	-	-	-
Crewton	-	-	-	-	-	-	-	-
Darley Abbey	324	-	-	1059	1000	945	915	676†
Dunkirk & St Luke's	400	-	-	-	-	-	11000	11767
Litchurch & Rose Hill	704	-	-	855	-	19,716†	-	-
Little Chester	436	-	-	364	-	571	-	7599
Little City	-	-	-	-	-	-	-	-
Little Eaton	552	395	507	-	692	946	992	1261
Littleover	1483	-	-	497	551	776	1385	3387‡
Mackworth	1383	409	621	561	510	1053	1450	3208
Markeaton	1912	-	-	200	-	758	199	-
Mickleover	4752	-	1144	1673	1809	1413	2084	3685‡
New Normanton	-	-	-	48	2750	2970	6771	-
New Zealand	-	-	-	-	-	-	-	6911
Normanton-by-Derby	1362	314	295	309	-	854	3780	9938
Ockbrook #	1730	829	1634	1765	1763	1938	2567‡	2971‡
Osmaston-by-Derby	1267	114	172	178	-	141	-	-
Pear Tree	-	-	-	-	-	-	6930	-
Quarndon	960	-	-	557	529	555	419	404‡
Rowditch & California	-	-	-	-	-	-	8045	-
Shelton Lock	-	-	-	-	-	-	-	-
Sinfin	1292	-	-	79	-	124	50	80
Spondon	3091	-	-	1586	2052	1757	2544	4881
Stenson	1120	-	-	115	-	104	69	71
Strutt's Park	75	-	-	-	-	-	-	-
West End	48	-	-	-	-	-	-	29780
Wilmorton	-	-	-	-	-	-	-	1981

Population figure includes Borrowash.
† Figure when absorbed by Derby, 1877.
‡ Population outside Borough.

Population of Derby as a Whole 1788-1951

Year	Population	Area(acres)
1788	8,563	-
1801	10,832	-
1811	13,043	-
1821	17,423	1840 (fixed by Mr Swanwick 1819)
1831	23,627	-
1841	32,741	1660
1851	40,609	-
1861	43,091	-
1871	49,810	-
1881	81,168	3324 Litchurch added 1878
1891	94,146	-
1901	105,912	3449 Boundary extension 1901
1911	123,410	-
1921	131,351	-
1931	142,403	5275
1951	141,264	8116

NB: Simpson, R. *History of Derby* (Derby, 3 vols.1826) III 851 quotes the population in 1377 as 1076 and in 1712 4000. The 1788 figure was computed by Pilkington, J. *History of Derbyshire* (Derby 1789) II 177.

Allenton

NAME: From Isaac Allen

ALLENTON is an example of a speculative piece of later nineteenth-century property development on a 'Green field' site within the parishes of Alvaston and Boulton. In the 1870s Isaac Allen was able to purchase several acres either side of the road from Derby to Swarkestone. In 1878 he began to build brick artisans' houses and, by 1895, there were five streets with another one under construction. In 1903 there were 150 houses. Allen also built the Crown Hotel in 1891 at a cost of £1,200, and it was here in April 1895 that the ossified remains of an extinct variety of hippopotamus (now in Derby Museum) were found; the skull, however, is still missing! Nor has this been the only important artifact from the suburb. In 1959 an iron axe-head of Viking type was found in a local garden, and fifteen years later a neolithic stone axe-hammer was also recovered.

Allen's first houses were offered for sale in the *Derby Mercury* 9 April 1879; by about 1890 a school had opened under the aegis of the Alvaston & Boulton School Board, and for a long time it was used on Sundays for church services. Part

The story of Allenton begins, really, with the Crown Inn built by Isaac Allen. The ossified remains of the hippopotamus were discovered whilst a well was being dug on the premises. Sir Henry Bemrose managed to obtain them for the Museum where they are still on display. Allen's executor's sold the inn to the Offiler family, as in this view of *c.*1921.

The youths of Allenton football club pose with great earnestness with cup and medals at the end of the 1926-27 season; from a postcard.

of the new suburb was incorporated into the Borough in 1901, and in 1925, after criticism from the Government for being slow to fulfil its Housing Act obligations, some of Derby's earliest council houses were erected here. Quite a number of these were prefabricated in cast iron, and the first of these were roofed in February 1926.

In 1928 the entire suburb became incorporated within the County Borough of Derby,

Osmaston Park Road, looking towards the 'Mitre' roundabout around 1948, well before the 'Spider Bridge' was erected . Note the blackout stripes still decorating the street lamp and trolley standards. The municipal housing here was built from 1925.

An early 1950s view, this time looking down Chellaston Road by the shops. Centre stage is taken by the Allenton Cinema, by this date renamed the Broadway (1939). It had been built to designs by T.H.Thorpe of Derby and opened with *Charley's Aunt* 17 December 1928. It closed with the instantly forgettable *Tommy the Toreador* on 24 September 1960 and was pulled down the following year to be replaced by Fine Fare. L.9799

enabling the Borough Council to make a start on the Arterial Road (later the Ring Road). This passed north of the centre of Mr Allen's village, the crossing with Chellaston Road being marked by a large new inn the Mitre – in 'Stockbroker's Tudor' style designed by T.H.Thorpe

of Derby for Zachary Smith's brewery, Shardlow, and opened in 1930. Either side of the Ring Road at Allenton more municipal housing was swiftly built, the resulting estate spreading across still-defined boundaries into Boulton, Alvaston and Osmaston. From this time, the houses built between the Mitre and the Crown began to be extended out across their gardens and converted into shops. In 1930, too, came the opening by Mrs J.P. Houlton of the new Wesleyan Chapel (opposite the Crown), a new cinema and, by 1934, a Municipal Secondary School had also been completed. In 1961 the open-air market (opened by the Mayor, Alderman Andrews) began making its vivid contribution to Allenton.

As traffic has grown, both on the road south through Allenton and around the Ring Road, so the provision of housing increased, fuelling a vicious circle of

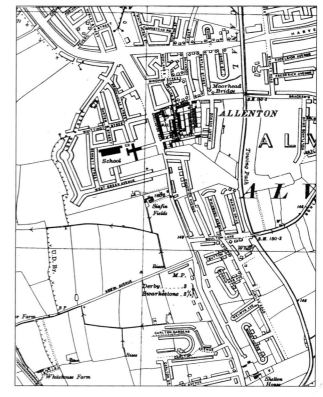

Allenton Market was opened in April 1961 and then consisted of 90 stalls. The original prospectus tells us that it was 'attractively roofed in coloured asbestos butterfly sheeting'! The photograph shows one of the sides – that nearest the Mitre – with trading in full swing not long after opening in summer 1961.

overcrowded roads and polluted air. One solution was the construction of an elevated pedestrian walkway over the traffic island at the Mitre – the so-called Spider Bridge – in 1971. Nevertheless, the problems remain, although over the last six or so years many municipal houses have been sold to their tenants and improved and those remaining in council ownership extensively refurbished.

Further reading:
Craven, M. *Illustrated History of Derbyshire* (Breedon, Derby 1988) 203, 215

Allestree

NAME: (Saxon) = Aedelheard's Tree/boundary marker.

I T WOULD appear that, prior to the Norman Conquest the village – if village is the correct word for the tiny scattered settled area then – was part of the holdings of Siward, Earl of Northumbria. By 1086, the completion of Domesday Book, it was a berewick – an outlier – of the Manor of Markeaton held by Hugh d'Avranches, Earl of Chester. Jocelyn, the Earl's steward and ancestor of the Touchet family of Markeaton, held the estate under him and Colle held parts in his turn from Jocelyn. Colle and his descendants appear to have later formed an alliance with Jocelyn's posterity and were quintessentially a Derby family.

By *c.*1135/1160 the Touchets had sold and granted much of the land of Allestree to Canons of the newly-founded Abbey of St Mary, Darley, renting a good deal back from the Abbey thereafter. So many charters of the Abbey survive detailing individual land-holdings that a detailed account could probably be compiled. By this time, too, a church, dedicated to St Edmund, had been founded at Allestree; the very fine surviving Norman doorcase of the church (totally rebuilt by Derby architect Henry Isaac Stevens in 1867) clearly attests to this. Doubtless it was founded by Henry de Touchet son of Jocelyn, but

Duffield Road, trolley bus no.219 (a Sunbeam F4 built 1952-53) emerges from the turn-round in Kingscroft *en route* to Alvaston (Wynham Street) via the town centre c.1962. This feature at Kingscroft was created in 1947 when the trolley bus route was extended from Broadway that September.

had come under the patronage of the Abbey by *c*.1190. Early in the next century the Abbey gave the chapel 4.5d annually to maintain a light at the feast of St Edmund there.

It is clear from a charter of 1208 that Richard son of Robert de Allstrey was a major freeholder of land in Allestree. He was quite possibly a direct descendant of Colle. One of his kinsmen, however, William son of Alice of Allestrey, was clearly not free, being given as his villein by Robert de Touchet 'with all his brood and his chattels' to the Abbey in the 1240s; Robert's brother Simon confirms this, also naming William de Allestrey's son Elias. Happily, in a charter of about a decade later the Abbot liberates Elias and Felicia his wife, settling them on three acres of the Abbey's land. It was Elias' descendants who went on to found an important Derby family some of whose descendants still live in the city.

Despite this, there is evidence that man was living in Allestree well over a millennium

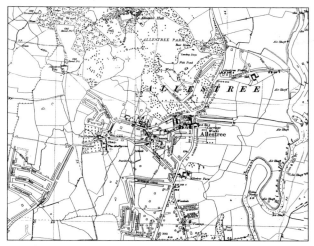

earlier, for an early Bronze Age tanged and barbed arrowhead was found in a garden in the 1970s. Twelfth to fourteenth-century pottery has been found in several places as well.

At the Reformation, most of Allestree was acquired by the Mundy family of Markeaton, and remained with them until the agricultural improver F.N.C. Mundy sold all but 10% of his holdings in the village to the financier and Darley Abbey mill owner Thomas Evans in the 1780s.

The old hall, in which the junior Mundys lived vanished at a slightly earlier time in the eighteenth century, but on the sale of some of Evans' land to Bache Thornhill of Stanton,

One of the most important elements of the Allestree Hall estate was the home farm, Allestree Farm, being the unit which serviced the 'in hand' part of the estate. The splendid brick house with its fine Regency bow was erected c.1805 to designs of James Wyatt (1746-1813). It managed to survive the break-up of the estate in 1928 (when it was farmed by William B.Woodisse) and the subsequent building on parts of the park. Ultimately, the coming of Abbey Hill doomed it, and it was cleared away to form a housing estate in 1972. L.6845

A view of the outbuildings of Allestree Farm just after the construction of the Abbey Hill roundabout, seen from the rather isolated apartments (Tudor Court) on the south-east side. Since this view was taken c.1970, the A38 extension has led to yet more great changes, although by that time Allestree Farm had long gone.

A number 11 trolley bus awaits passengers on Kedleston Road by the corner of Allestree Lane in the 1950s. Bus no.179 was a Sunbeam W chassis with a Park Royal body as delivered in 1946. It was scrapped in 1965. Route 11 ran from Allestree Lane to the Midland Station. On the right is the misleadingly-named Markeaton Hotel (well, it overlooked Markeaton state land) by Naylor and Sale, opened 13 May 1938.

a new one was begun in 1802 to a much-revised design of James Wyatt and finished a few years later for John Girardot, an East-Indian merchant turned local vintner. By the 1820s, however, a branch of the Evans family had acquired that, too. On its sale in the 1920s the parkland was acquired to build housing and as a golf course. Fortunately, the war stopped the housing going beyond Main, Short and Evans Avenues.

Drawing of Allestree Vicarage, 1890s. This splendid house was designed by Henry Isaac Stevens of Derby and built in 1866-67, as part of Stevens' refurbishment of the parish church.

The Methodist Chapel was built in 1895, and by 1936 the largest landowner was Commercial Constructions Ltd – a bad omen! There were 1,412 residents in 1931. Most of the village however was not absorbed by Derby until 1968. This was the signal for considerable developments on land on the west side of the village. Birchover Way had already provided the spine of a colossal development, expanding from earlier private building off Allestree Lane. A new shopping centre was started in 1962 called Park Farm, complete with tower block (one of only two residential ones in the city) and was finished by 1968. It was extended again in 1972-73.

Further reading:

Allen, J.W.	*Allestree from Adelard to Raphael* (Derby 1975)
Bailey, G.	*Reminiscences of Old Allestree* (Derbyshire Archaeological Journal VII (1885) 168F.
Boyes, M.	*Allestree Hall* (Derby 1982)
Burdis, F.	*In Those Days, Memories of Bygone Allestree* (Derby 1970)
Eisenberg, E.	*Allestree* (Derby n.d. c.1980s).
Lucas, R.	*The Manor of Markeaton, Mackworth and Allestree 1650-1851* (Derby 1995)
Ward, J.T.	*Reminiscences of Allestree* (Derby 1934)

Alvaston

Name: 'The farm of Aethelwald', first recorded AD1002.

ALVASTON certainly existed by 1002, in which year the Saxon thegn Wulfric Spot left it (and many other places) to his kinsman Wulfheah (son of Ealdorman Aelfhelm of Southern Northumbria, probably by Wulfric's sister). Man had, however, been on the site from at least the early Bronze Age, for a small flint of this era was found in a local garden in 1977.

At the Norman Conquest the thegn Toki held Alvaston – perhaps a descendant of the fortunate Wulfheah – but by 1086 when Domesday was published, he had been displaced by the Norman Geoffrey Alselin who held it along with Ambaston, Thulston and Elvaston as a single manorial estate. There was a church, a fact confirmed by the discovery of a Saxon coffin-lid in the fabric of the medieval church when the ubiquitous Henry Isaac Stevens was 'restoring' St Michael's in 1856. The manor continued amongst Alselin's

A view of Alvaston Street looking towards the church of St Michael and All Angels, with a pair of well-heeled locals gossiping in the morning sun. On the right the ancient premises of Joseph Holder, a long-established chimney sweep. The church was totally rebuilt by Henry Isaac Stevens of Derby (1807-1873) in 1856-57, the previous church – an Anglo-Saxon foundation – having much mid-fourteenth-century fabric and a tower rebuilt (possibly by Joseph Pickford) in 1772. L11886

descendants until it was granted by one of them to the Abbot of Dale. The church, on the other hand, was allied to and part of the Derby parish of St Michael, granted to the Abbey of Darley, along with some land at Alvaston.

The Sacheverell family held the Abbey of Dale's lands and obtained them after the Reformation. Likewise, the descendants of Elias de Allestrey, whom we met under Allestree, were tenants of Darley Abbey of that monastery's land at Alvaston. Before the end of the sixteenth century, the Allestreys had bought much of the Sacheverell lands and later acquired from the Borough the patronage of the church, too.

Another Alvaston Street building – almost as venerable as the medieval church – was the cottage seen on the right of the previous view. It had a timber-framed core with three intact medieval crucks. A campaign was mounted to save it, but to no avail. This view was one of many taken as part of a survey of the building on 25 February 1938. It was demolished the following month. L182

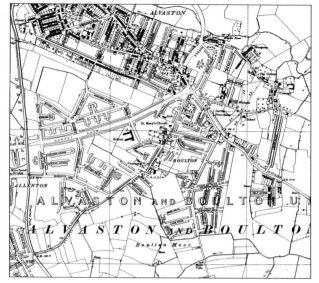

The Poplars is one of the important group of Regency villas which still survive in and around Derby. It was built in the late 1820s on the corner of Elvaston Lane and Church Street. From the 1850s until 1952 it was the home of the Smiths, coachbuilders at Derby. Maud and Dorothy, daughters of Herbert Dagley Smith (1845-1914) are probably the ladies visible in this 1900s postcard view. On the side of the house is visible a cast-iron decorative escutcheon bearing *a lion rampant*; it is still there.

They also built Alvaston Hall and dominated the life of the village until the senior line died out in 1741 and the Borough family took over, selling off much land. By the nineteenth century several pleasant villas set in considerable grounds had been built, and towards the end of that century the village was beginning to expand, one part – Crewton (qv.) – being carved out of the parish completely.

On 25 March 1884 Alvaston was merged with Boulton (qv.) as a single civil parish, both having been governed by the same local board from 1851. In 1894 a new Urban District Council was set up and remained responsible for Alvaston until 1934, except for those parts of the village absorbed by Derby Corporation in 1901 (basically Crewton) and again (much of the rest) in 1928. The church became centre of a separate parish in 1865. Baptist and Methodist Chapels were built in the nineteenth century and in the present one a striking Roman Catholic Church. The remainder of Alvaston passed to Derby in 1934 and outlying portions in 1968.

From 1880 a horse bus served Alvaston (Harrington Arms), replaced by electric trams from 27 July 1904. This service was itself replaced by trolley buses which ran to Wyndham Street off Harvey Road from 14 July 1932. The coming of the Ring Road was made possible by the Borough extensions and virtually divided Alvaston in two. Post-war development has continued, especially over the last decade south-east of Coronation Avenue along Shardlow Road, and with the new Stoke-Derby Link Road spur coming in nearby, will probably continue.

Alvaston is also notorious for the first recorded local sighting of a UFO (or, possibly, comet) and the second recorded local earthquake. The latter was reported in the *Derby Mercury* on 5 October 1750. The former was witnessed by Nicholas de Findern of Findern

and 'a large number of people'. Apparently in the early evening a 'bright star' appeared out of a black cloud in an otherwise clear sky. Two other 'stars' appeared alongside it and apparently 'charged' the first one repeatedly causing 'sparks' to fall. The larger star began to diminish in size. This continued until the crowd 'stupefied by fear and ignorant of what it might portend' fled. All this in the mid-thirteenth century!

Sometime around *c.*1860 a new tollhouse was erected on the London Road, approximately on the southern boundary of Derby. The result was surprisingly stylish, and still survives, thanks to a major refurbishment carried out a decade or so ago. The turnpike trust, however, was wound up in 1888. L12433

A postcard of *c.*1904 showing the point, on Shardlow Road, Alvaston, where Boulton Lane (then more commonly called Boulton Street) debouched. On the left, the pleasure grounds of Mr C.H.Soresby's elegant Nunsfield House (built 1828), today probably the only structure apart from the church to survive in this area today. When Harvey Road was built from 1929 the cottages were quickly pulled down. L1772

Further reading:
Craven, M.   *Illustrated History of Derby* (Breedon 1988) 163, 183, 196, 215, 217.
Craven, M. & Stanley, M.   *The Derbyshire Country House* Vol.II (Matlock 1984) 13

A postcard view almost certainly taken on the same day as the preceding, and certainly by the same photographer, showing the houses out of shot on the right of the picture of Boulton Lane end. It is London Road (Shardlow Road) Alvaston looking north. Today the scene is of a dual carriageway road, two roundabouts and shops.

Only a few years on, and urbanisation is already taking a grip on London Road, Alvaston. The real catalyst was the coming of the electric trams as far as the Harrington Arms Inn from 27 July 1904. Here, nearby, a procession mounted to mark the funeral of King Edward VII in 1910 is passing.

A later view of The Triangle (see p24) of *c*.1936. Where, in that view there was just grass and trees, now municipal houses line the road. The Triangle itself had acquired seats, and a chain link fence. The Harvey Road trolley bus service started on 24 July 1932. From a postcard. L2582

Once the 1928 Borough Extension Act had become law, sufficient of Osmaston, Boulton and Alvaston parishes had become part of the County Borough of Derby to enable a start to be made on the Arterial Road – the Ring Road – from 1929. This view, looking towards Beech Avenue, Alvaston is from newly-completed Harvey Road, about February 1931. On the right the new entrance to Boulton Lane. Ahead a triangular junction has been made with Shardlow Road known appropriately as – The Triangle! L2196

A few yards further north was the junction with Raynesway, the last element of the Ring Road to be built before the outbreak of World War Two, 1937-39. This view of the new junction dates from around 1938. The total absence of traffic is truly awesome!

About a year earlier, this view, taken by Hurst & Wallis, shows London Road from what was in due time to become Raynesway. The red flag and a board (right centre) was sufficient to deter motorists from entering the far-from-finished thoroughfare. L2188

The Alvaston sector of Raynesway is pictured looking west in the early 1950s. New factories are beginning to spring up along the still-new road with its dual carriageway, footpaths and cycle tracks. Yet apart from an Austin A40 van, the entire scene is again devoid of traffic!

The Alvaston cinema was built in London Road to designs by Thomas Harrison Thorpe of Derby and opened with *Decameron Nights* on 2 March 1925. The design was taken as the basis for the Allenton cinema. On 10 August 1939 it was renamed the Rex, but closed after the showing of *Seven Brides for Seven Brothers* on 22 October 1966. This view was taken as recently as November 1982 when it was for sale. It was demolished for a caravan showroom 9-11 July 1983.

After the war, and after the building restrictions which followed, the erection of municipal housing around Harvey Road, begun in 1929, resumed. This is a view of newly-completed housing on Garrick Street taken in the late 1950s.

Right: On the same occasion, this view of Thorndike Avenue (from Garrick Street) was taken. The front gardens lack all maturity, suggesting that they had been planted little more than a year or so.

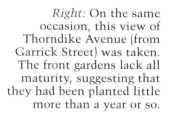

Boulton

Name: 'The farm of Bola' – Saxon origin.

BOULTON first occurs in the Domesday Book (1086). Then, the manor belonged to a Norman grandee called Ralph FitzHubert of Crich, who had displaced one Leofnoth, a Saxon, and installed Colle as undertenant, whom we have already met as Jocelyn's undertenant at Allestree. He also held land at Youlgreave.

Boulton was never a large place and its border with Alvaston was never wholly clear. However it was an integral part of the parish of St Peter, Derby, as Alvaston

Two scenes taken in Boulton Lane at about the turn of the century – quite probably on the same occasion as the view which appears under Alvaston, of its junction with Shardlow Road. It is all still wonderfully bucolic, but all about to change. L9112, L12716

The housing, both municipal and private, which began to march across the former Nunsfield and Alvaston Fields estates before World War Two, was stopped in its tracks in 1939. After the peace in 1945, there were serious building restrictions, so that work did not resume until the late 1940s. This 1946 view of the incomplete Rosedale Avenue, looking west-north-west towards the backs of the council houses lining Harvey Road illustrates the hiatus graphically. Many houses were built of artificial stone blocks called The Stanley Block marketed by a Chaddesden builder called T.H.Anthony. L2192

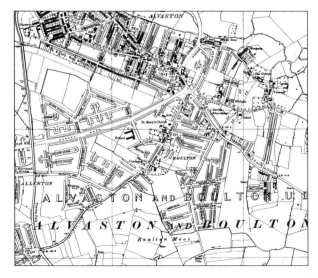

had been with that of St Michael, and was thus anciently esteemed a parcel of the Borough.

FitzHubert's tenants were a family who took their name from the place, but by the 1180s Boulton passed (probably by marriage) to the Sacheverells, who shortly afterwards acquired their land in Alvaston (qv) thus adding to the difficulty of distinguishing the two settlements apart. Darley Abbey were patrons of St Peter's Derby, the mother church, and hence acquired land in Boulton, too.

The south doorway of the church is

A view taken on the same day as the preceding is this of the housing halted in its advance across Boulton Moor: Strathmore Avenue, semi-complete, Rosslyn Gardens is the turning, left, middle distance. The house on the right can be seen in the left background of the previous view. L2189

Norman, which suggests that it existed by the twelfth century: the chancel arch was also Norman, but was destroyed in 1840 when John Mason of Derby enlarged it. It was and is dedicated to the Blessed Virgin Mary, and was extended again in 1871, 1887 and 1907. Otherwise there are vestiges of fabric of practically all eras within. It became a separate parish in 1730.

Like Alvaston, the parish was enclosed in 1802 and governed from 1851 by a local board, replaced by an Urban District Council in 1894. Much of Boulton was absorbed by Derby in 1928 and the old UDC was wound up six years later. The reintegration of Boulton with Derby enabled a crucial part of the Ring Road (Derby Arterial Road) to be constructed from Osmaston Park to Alvaston at Shardlow Road – today's Harvey Road. From 1928, too, large amounts of municipal housing were constructed mainly on either side of Harvey Road, supplemented by further extensive additions to the stock of council houses around Boulton Lane, Holbrook Road (named after the builder of Nunsfield House) and Brackens Lane, the latter named after a vanished farm.

A view of the similarly incomplete Holloway Road taken once building had restarted in the early 1950s. The school, centre, is Boulton, Wyndham Street, built in the early 1930s. L2157

The only houses of any substance were Nunsfield House and Alvaston Fields – the latter built by the heir of the Allestrey family, J.T.Borough, to replace Alvaston Hall – and it was in part the break-up of their modest estates that enabled Derby corporation to acquire so much land to carry out their building programme.

Further reading:
Craven, M. *Illustrated History of Derby* (Breedon 1988) 215, 221

Breadsall

NAME: 'Braegd's corner of land' – Anglo-Saxon, including the same personal name as Breaston, not far away.

IN 1002 Breadsall was given to Burton Abbey by Wulfric Spot, but by 1066 a Norse-descended thegn called Siward held it along with eight other manors, all of which had passed by 1086 to Henry de Ferrers. There was, even then, a church and a mill, and it was held under Ferrers by one Robert Dun, whose descendants held it into the thirteenth century.

The heiress of this family divided the manor into two distinct holdings, Breadsall Nether Hall (now partly occupied by Oakwood) and Breadsall Over Hall or Upper Hall. The latter passed to a branch of the Curzon family, from whom it was inherited by the Dethicks. The remains of their manor house – one of the most ancient in Derbyshire – still stand, much restored, serving community purposes, opposite the church. From the Dethicks it passed c.1600 to John Harpur, a younger son of the powerful Harpurs of Swarkestone. His heirs, the Harpur-Crewes, still own some property in the village today, although much was disposed of some thirty years ago.

The church, an important one spanning the thirteenth to fifteenth centuries with a Norman south door of c.1150, is dedicated to All Saints. It was restored in 1830 and again

Breadsall has suffered from being divided by the expansion of Derby. The core of the old village is still just outside the City's boundary, but the former Borough Council were able to acquire the Hill Top, Mount and Priory Flatte estates up until 1968, along with land once (to 1926) attached to the Chaddesden Hall estate of the Wilmots. This 1890s view of the church and old village was made into a postcard c.1904.

in 1877-86 and re-dedicated after the fire (qv.) 14 April 1916. The rectory (now called the Manor) is yet another of Derby's fine Regency villas, built in 1836 for Revd Henry Robert

The Breadsall Nether Hall and Priory estates escaped the grasp of the Borough Council (thanks to continuing private ownership) – and hence the survival of the old village. This view of the Old Hall and part of the church towards Moor Road was taken in the heat of 22 August 1968. L3389/N

A Richard Keene photograph taken in the 1870s of old cottages in Rectory Lane Breadsall, from a glass slide. Then the homes of agricultural labourers, today they have been sold by the Harpur-Crewe estate and converted into bijou residences for well-heeled commuters.

Once upon a time – to be precise, between 1876 and 1968 – the Ilkeston-Egginton Junction branch of the former Great Northern Railway ran through Breadsall. This winter, late morning view shows a pair of local residents on the Bridle Road from Brookside Road to the main road by the Windmill Inn as it went under the line. Brookside Road is behind the camera in this 1926 view. L11268

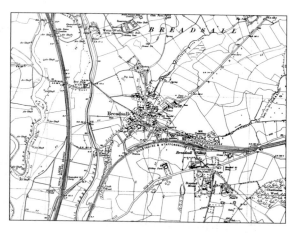

On Moor Road stands the old village school, photographed in full use in 1968. It was built in 1837 at the expense of Sir John Harpur-Crewe Bt. in a *cottage orne* style and was probably designed and built by Thomas Cooper of Derby who had been responsible for the palatial rectory of 1832. L3390/N

(Harpur) Crewe (rector 1830-1865) by the 8th Baronet to designs by Thomas Cooper of Derby (1787-1850). It has since been secularised and is now the home of Sir Richard and Lady Morris.

Some time before 1266 a Priory of Augustinian Friars was established by the Curzons on part of their estate in the north of the Parish. This was dissolved in 1536, after which it was replaced by a country house and estate, most notably associated (albeit briefly) with Erasmus Darwin FRS who died there 18 April 1802. Later the seat of the Haslams of Derby (see Strutt's Park) – it is now an hotel with golf course and country club.

Several other large houses were built on the higher part of the parish in the nineteenth century, when much of the area was owned by the Sacheverells' heirs the Batemans of Morley, most notably Breadsall Mount, from 1927 the Bishop's Palace for Derby Diocese. Although Breadsall was never anciently part of Derby, a portion was transferred to Little Eaton (which had been) in 1934, and other parts – Breadsall Hill Top – passed to Derby Corporation, supplemented by a great deal more of the parish in 1868.

This, along with land sales by the Batemans, enabled the Corporation of Derby to begin expanding their Chaddesden estate over the hill and almost into Little Chester. After World War Two, building began on the Hill Top and St Andrew's View estates.

A central part of the ancient village settlement, of course, was its largely thirteenth-century church, graced by its soaring early fourteenth-century spire. A Norman doorcase survives to attest its antiquity and until 1914 there was some superb early carved oak. However all the latter (and much more) was destroyed in a serious fire in 1914 allegedly started by militant supporters of women's suffrage. The photograph was taken by F.W.Scarratt a day or two later. The church was subsequently restored with great sensitivity by W.D.Caroe (1857-1938). Inset: a postcard view of the church actually burning.

The modern suburb of Oakwood – unlike the others not municipally owned – was carved out of the parish in the 1970s.

The Derby Canal (Little Eaton branch) of 1796 partly crossed the parish, and the Great Northern Railway line from Ilkeston to Derby passed through from 1877, the company building a station at Breadsall (closed thirty years ago) in the process.

Ancient man has left us with Peg Low – a mound of unknown date in a field south-west of the rectory; a possible stretch of Roman Road with some Roman Derbyshire Ware in Porter Lane (1956) and a Neolithic stone mace head of quartzite was found in 1973.

Breadsall, of course, has a western boundary which marches with Little Chester, which is why this postcard of the Borough Infectious Diseases Hospital is marked 'Little Chester'. The drive left the Mansfield Road by the bridge which carried the later over the Little Eaton branch of the Derby Canal. This is the west side of the hospital, built in 1890 and photographed about a decade later. It was designed by R.J.Harrison and built as four separate blocks on a six acre site. Photograph by F.W.Scarratt.

A more recent view of the hospital, of 1960, when it had become the Derwent Hospital. It was somewhat rebuilt in the 1930s by Charles Aslin, as seen here, and after closure in 1985 was demolished a year later, and the site being given over to housing. L862

The Breadsall Hill Top estate was largely built on in the 1950s, and extended on to the site of Breadsall Mount, a nineteenth-century county house acquired by the then Borough from the Diocese of Derby in 1968. Building, as here, in St Andrew's View, began almost immediately. This photograph was taken c.1970, from Grantham Avenue, showing the junior school. The area (and a street) were called St Andrew's View because the old railway church of that name on London Road, Derby, was easily the most prominent distant feature to be seen; except that, by the time the housing was complete, Sir Gilbert Scott's fine church had been demolished (in 1970)! L2154/N

Further reading:

Cox, J.C.	*The Destruction of All Saints' Church, Breadsall* in Derbyshire Archaeological Journal XXXVII (1915) 127
Currey, P.H.	*The Priory (Breadsall)* in Derbyshire Archaeological Journal XXVII (1905) 127
Kerry, C.	*Early Breadsall Charters* in Derbyshire Archaeological Journal XVI (1894) 157
Newton, J.	*The Story of Breadsall Church* (Derby 1966)

Burnaston

Name: 'Brunwulf's farm', Old English (1086)

small settlement within the parish of Etwall, Burnaston was, with Bearwardcote, divided into no less than five manors, held before 1066 by five individual Anglo-Saxon noblemen. After 1087, however, it was all Henry de Ferrers'.

By the early seventeenth century, the Bonnington family owned the Burnaston portions, later selling to the Sleighs of Etwall. In 1820, Ashton Mosley acquired the township and built a new house (the previous, seventeenth century, seat, Burnaston Old Hall being in the village) to designs by Francis Goodwin. After various changes in ownership, house and 382 acres of the estate were purchased by Derby Borough Council in 1936 in order to make a municipal aerodrome. The cost was £21,500. This was opened by Sir Kingsley Wood PC, MP three years later, with the house in use as a clubhouse and terminal building.

In 1968 the airport's main functions were taken over by East Midlands Airport, and the airfield declined into one dedicated to club flying only, and the house was sold and decayed. In 1989 it

Burnaston, despite the ugly scar of Toyota's works rising on the former Mosley Burnaston House estate, has never been within the City boundary. Yet in 1936 Derby did acquire the self-same Burnaston House estate on which to build its new municipal aerodrome, opened on 17 June 1939. This is a 1954 view of the control tower with Francis Goodwin's elegant villa of 1826 behind. The latter was used as the club house and terminal. The airport lost its role, bar some club flying, when East Midlands opened in 1968. The house was sold and all was swept away for car manufacturing from 1990. L271

was resolved to offer the site to Messrs Toyota as a car manufacturing facility, and in 1990 the house was pulled down – being dismantled and stored (and is still available for re-erection) and the new factory was begun, producing its first cars 3½ years later. From 1989, however, Derby's control over this 40 acre 'suburb' ceased for the time being.

Further reading:
Anon.,   *Derby's Airport,* commemorative Programme (Derby 1939)
Craven, M.   *Illustrated History of Derby* (Breedon 1988) 215-16, 224-25
Craven, M. & Stanley, M.   *The Derbyshire Country House* (Breedon, Derby 1991) 48-49

California

Name: See below.

THIS district could be said to lie south of the former GNR Derby (Friar Gate) to Egginton Junction railway line, north of the Littleover Brook, east of Rough Heanor and west of Rowditch, mainly in the former parishes of Mackworth and Littleover. It is marked on OS maps from about the 1880s, but not on the engraved maps of Swanwick and Rogerson (both 1819). It would be reasonable to assume that the name was coined as a result of the California (USA) gold rush of 1849, but why it should apply to this area is quite unclear. There was not even a farm bearing this name in the area.

A wonderful aerial shot of this enigmatic area of Derby, showing the newly-finished Ring Road – Kingsway and, in the distance, right, Queensway – with the Kingsway Hospital in the left foreground. In the middle distance is another of Derby's Regency villas, Thornhill of 1821. By this time it was inhabited by two of Sir Oswald Mosley's aunts. Now it is dilapidated and threatened. Across Kingsway is Thornhill Farm and Rowditch Brickworks, now the site of Sainsbury's and other out-of-town stores. Beyond the GNR route from Friar Gate to Mickleover is Wallace Street with New Zealand Square to its west, newly completed, dating the view to about 1935.

Until the Borough extension of 1901, little development took place except on part of the Thornhill estate. Thorn Hill was the highest part of the area, and the Knoll which bore this name has been embellished, since 1821, by a stuccoed Regency villa of some size built by Alderman Richard Leaper (1759-1838) for the Long Eaton mill pioneer Col. John Trowell. Later it became a residence for Sir Oswald Mosley's aunts before being taken over by the Derby Lunatic Asylum, adjacent. The NHS are currently running it down and its fate hangs in the balance.

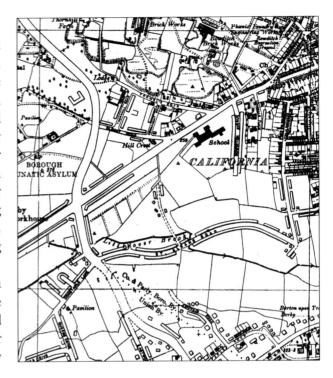

After 1928 the Ring Road was built in a great sweep through the area and more housing, some municipal, appeared between the Ring Road and Uttoxeter Road. Some of the latter is now extremely run down.

The area west of Thornhill was used to build a temporary isolation hospital and later the Union Workhouse (by Giles and Brookhouse 1877, demolished 1989) as well of the Borough Asylum. Later, in 1931, the City Hospital was added, and, like the DRI, has been expanding ever since. The land to the east of the Ring Road (here called Kingsway) was a tip until the 1970s when it was stabilised and in the following decade Messrs Sainsbury's was built thereon, followed by an inn – the King's Highway – and in the 1990s more 'superstores'. Thornhill is to be covered by cheap housing; the Workhouse site – latterly Manor Hospital – is now covered by apartments and a 'motel' and pub/restaurant called the Mallard. Also, the fire station moved to the area from Willow Row in the early 1960s.

It is not easy to distinguish where California's boundaries are, particularly with Rowditch to the east.

Chaddesden

Name: 'The Valley of Ceadd', the second element deriving from Anglo-Saxon *denn* (Valley) rather than *dun/tun* (farm).

DOMESDAY Book (1086) omits to mention who held the sokeland at Chaddesden (it did not then rate manorial status) before the Norman conquest, but it was part of Henry de Ferrers' 112 Derbyshire manors by then.

The church appeared later, dedicated to St Mary, as a Chapelry of Spondon. It owes its existence, almost certainly, to the munificence of the subtenants of the Duchy of Cornwall (as successors of the disgraced Ferrers), the de Chaddesden family, and was founded some time between 1291 and 1347. In 1362, Henry de Chaddesden (d.1354), Archdeacon of Leicester, by his will, established quite an opulent chantry at the church supported by part of the family estate. Most of the church seems to date from c.1357 with additions over the following century, and is important as a rare dated example before the mid-

Parish Church of St Mary, Chaddesden Lane photographed c.1900 from the south-east by Charles Barrow Keene and later turned into a postcard. An earlier church was completely rebuilt in 1357-58 and the inevitable nineteenth-century restoration was undertaken exactly 500 years later with considerable tact by C.Place and G.E.Street. In this view, for instance, the east window is their work. L3294

The church stands at the east side of Chaddesden Lane, the lower part of which is shown in this view of c.1931. The houses here were built along the western edge of the Chaddesden Hall park after the latter's sale by the Wilmot family in 1926. L11338

Beyond the church, which marked the north-west limit of the hall park, Chaddesden Lane jinks round to the east by the Wilmot Arms from whence it becomes Morley Road. The sale of the hall and estate also released land here for building. This 1934 view shows bungalows, a not-very-old motor vehicle, and an example of the old cast-iron road signs – in this case to denote the new village school built to the designs of G.H.Widdows a year before. L11337

fifteenth century (cf. Spondon). The chunky embattled three stage tower dates from the same period. It was rather insensitively restored in 1849-59 by George O'Brien and again, with some decorum, in 1904 by G.F.Bodley.

After the extinction of the Chaddesden family c.1400 the land was divided amongst three families (presumably through heiresses), although by 1626 when the Wilmots from Derby had built their hall beside the church, having acquired the lion's share,

The extension of the Borough's boundaries in 1928 enabled the Corporation to at last control enough vacant land around the periphery of the town to commence building the Derby Arterial Road (A5111) later known as the Ring Road. The part from Alvaston to Chaddesden was one of the most challenging, crossing as it did the Derwent, the London Midland & Scottish Railway and the canal. It was completed in 1939 and ultimately named after Alderman William Robert Raynes (1870-1966) one of the first Labour councillors, the first Labour Mayor (in 1921-22) and MP 1923-24 and 1929-31. L2198

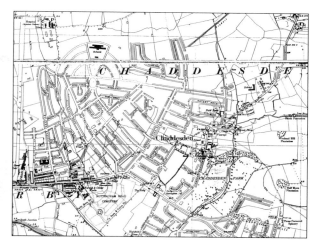

Left: The difficult crossing of the Derwent was made close to Alvaston. This view is from the decking of the steel bridge, looking towards Alvaston, 1938. L2198

Below: Another view, showing the entire bridge from the northern bank of the Derwent. The later sections of the Derby Arterial Road were dual carriageway; the earlier ones were not, cf. Osmaston Park Road. L2198

The crossing over the railway was just as challenging as that over the Derwent because the road had to cross not only the main line (left), but also the Chaddesden spur (centre) and the Derby Canal (right). This photograph was taken in winter 1938, looking west towards Chaddesden Sidings. L2199

The same bridge from the other side looking east, showing it complete with its brick and concrete cladding, April 1939 the chimney (left) belonged to Leech Neal & Co's paintworks. Spondon Jc. signal box to the right of it. L2199

including the patronage of the church which had become a perpetual accuracy. Only in modern times has it become a vicarage. The Wilmots dominated the village despite the pretensions of the Newtons and the Cokaynes the former also built almshouses (qv.) numerous cottages and the pub bearing their arms. Even as late as 1789 the village was operating a four course rotation of crops; fallow/wheat/barley/peas or beans – a leftover from medieval times. The ridge and furrow is still visible in the park (since 1926 a public open space) and near Raynesway.

Early man is represented by a barbed and flanged flint arrowhead found c.1973 and a coin of the first century Roman emperor Vespasian was found in a stream bank at about the same period; perhaps insufficient evidence to postulate a settlement, however!

The first school in the parish was founded in 1705; it was refounded by Robert Wilmot in 1736-37, but in the present century was demolished. A later school opposite Church Lane was also gone by 1958.

The Wilmots replaced their house in the 1720s but sold up in 1926 when the hall was destroyed and much of their estate and parkland became available for 'redevelopment'. Further, in 1901 Derby acquired part of Chaddesden to which a great deal more was added in 1928. The remainder was merged with Derby forty years later.

In 1796 the Canal (Erewash branch) had been built along the meadows at the foot of Chaddesden Hill, itself anciently in Derby. In 1854-55 this area became Derby's second cemetery and H.I.Stevens designed and built the attractive lodge and entrance. Slightly to the east the Midland Railway's loop line of 1840 was made the basis of a large complex of lines called Chaddesden Sidings and in the mid 1860s J.H.Sandars built Highfield Cottages nearby for the Midland Railway to house the workers, now one of Derby's newest Conservation Areas.

The first municipal houses were proposed as early as 1919, but it was not until after the

Raynesway Railway Bridge: view from the roadway looking south, April 1939. Note protected cycle track and footpath – all very 'state-of-the-art'! L2199

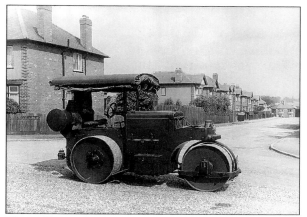

The effort of constructing Raynesway was not undertaken without mechanical assistance, of course! This photograph from July 1939 shows a lightweight Green's road roller posing at the junction of Chaddesden Park Road and Spinney Road after surfacing the latter. In the distance, Curzon Road O131.

Wilmot Estate was acquired that building began in earnest c.1929. The shopping area on Nottingham Road was developed then, too, the Chaddesden Park Hotel (since much renamed) being completed at about the same time by Naylor and Sale. After the war building continued apace, and new churches were required – St Mark's in Francis Street (1938) by Naylor & Sale again, St Philip's, Taddington Road (1954-55) by S.W.Milburn

Opposite the door of Chaddesden church once stood a group of six minuscule timber-framed almshouses built 1638-39. Part of a bequest of 16 (the other ten were in Derby's Bridge Gate), they formed Wilmot's Charity or the Black Hospital, the latter name deriving from the requirement that the inmates wore the livery of their benefactor, Robert Wilmot of Chaddesden Hall which was black trimmed silver. They provided shelter for four poor men and two poor women of the parish who received 1/- (5p) per week, increased in 1671 to 2/- (10p). There were two outside privies to serve all six houses. After a long battle and three years boarded up they were demolished in February 1963. This photograph was taken in 1959. L7876

Hillcrest Road, a misty February morning c.1951 reveals the depressing site of the former dairy of Hill Crest Farm quietly decaying, the fields on which once ran the herds that supplied it by no more than a decade past swamped with houses. From its appearance it would appear to date from the 1840s, and boasts cast-iron window frames. It probably represents contemporary improvements made to the Wilmot's estate.

As soon as the worst post-war building restrictions ended, local councils, Derby included, were able to resume their programmes of council house construction. This included the area bounded by Canterbury Street, Max Road and Wood Road. This view taken in early spring 1947 shows two distinct varieties of municipal housing being built on Grindlow Road looking north-west towards Matlock Road – the entire estate has its streets named after Derbyshire places. L2146, L12711

and for the Methodists in Chesapeake Road (1956) by T.H.Thorpe are examples. Trams from Derby reached the cemetery on 8 February 1908, but their demise came early, on 14 November 1930, when a motorbus was substituted, running to Lime Grove. However, by 9 January 1932 trolley bus route 66 was running as far as Nottingham Road Creamery (it was replaced by a motorbus from 11 November 1962 – just over 30 years later). Motorbuses also served Perth

A view taken a little later either in Cromford or Gertrude Road, looking back towards Wood Road, with road surfacing in full swing, the contractor being T.W.Annable of Shepshed. This photograph also gives a more detailed view of the aluminium clad houses (a type much favoured by the government of the day, keen to keep former aircraft factories in production). They were by no means wholly successful, and many have been subsequently sheathed in brick.

Street, Priory estate, Grindlow Road, Trenton Green and Alvaston from Nottingham Road Creamery via Raynesway.

Raynesway (qv.) was the last part of Derby's intended Ring Road to be built before World War Two. The final link thence to Broadway was never undertaken, but in the 1970s, a new extension of the A52 was built on the line of the canal to the bottom of Stores Road (which was complimented with the stretch from Sir Frank Whittle Way to Abbey Hill) which effectively forged the final link. Since then, Chaddesden Sidings have been redeveloped as an out-of-town shopping complex – called, after the Midland Railway Crest, Wyvern Park. It has been rounded off by the building of a 'motel' called the Travel Inn there in 1995 and the projected restoration of the canal (albeit on a slightly different alignment) is planned for 2000.

Further reading:

Craven, M.	*Illustrated History of Derby* (Breedon 1988) 44, 47, 138, 105-06, 220-21
Craven, M. & Stanley, M.	*The Derbyshire Country House* (Breedon 1991) 58-59
Fearneyhough, H. W.	*Chaddesden, A History* (Ashbourne, 1991)
Window, R.	*Some Notes on Chaddesden, in* Derbyshire Miscellany.

Chellaston

Name: 'The farm of Ceolheard' – Old English/Saxon, also attested on Chellaston Hill, Weston, as *Ceoleardsbeorge* 'The hill of Ceolheard'.

THE village is first attested in a Charter of 1009, when it is part of several adjacent places assigned to the manor of Melbourne to provide income for the Bishop of Carlisle, whose holding it was. As far as the Bishop was concerned, Melbourne was a bolt-hole to be retired to when border conflicts in his see became too hot for him. Thus 1.5 carucates of land at Chellaston (along with the later church) pertained to Melbourne until the 1860s when the whole of the village became a separate ecclesiastical parish served by a vicar instead of someone appointed by the incumbent of Melbourne. There was a separate manor in Chellaston, held in 1066, by the opulent Wulfsi (who also held Kedleston, Radbourne, Bradbourne, Risley and Weston Underwood) and yet another then under the control of Osmund of Osmaston. By 1086 Wulfsi's manor had been given to the Danish-sounding Amalric and Osmund retained his part after the conquest – a rare event.

The Bishop of Carlisle's portion (the largest) was sublet to a gentry family, and thus,

A mixed Board School was erected in Chellaston in 1878 at a cost of £2,000, for 150 children. This solemn group of children from one of the classes was part of the first intake, photographed in that same year with Mr Martin, one of the two staff members. Martin got a house with his new job and miraculously, both house and school survive today, one as a private residence the other as Chellaston Infants' School. Courtesy the late Cllr Ken Brown. L4462

The mining and working of alabaster from pits at Chellaston (and elsewhere in the Trent Valley, notably Fauld and Eston, Staffs), goes back at least to the fourteenth century. The soft milky coloured stone with its distinctive rusty stains was worked into ornaments great and small until as late as the 1960s when the industry died and the pits were filled in. Fine white alabaster was also crushed for gypsum, plaster of Paris and flooring. This view from the 1890s is of Pegg's quarry. Pegg & Co. had been founded in about 1850 by John Harpur, a brick manufacturer (see Dunkirk) and Alderman Robert Pegg (1801-1870), Mayor of Derby in 1855. He also founded a paint works, later Pegg & Ellam Jones. L5034

with the other two manors as well, the subsequent land ownership of the parish becomes confusing, to say the least.

The church is dedicated to St Peter, and its foundations may go back to Norman times, for this is the period of the font, although its base is later. The fabric of the church itself is partly c.1320 and partly late fifteenth century, including the chancel. The tower was added in 1842. Inside, there are many fine medieval and later monuments in the celebrated local alabaster which was mined in the parish from at least 1367 until the 1960s. It was not only carved, but was also used to produce gypsum and plaster-of-paris. Furthermore, crushed alabaster was also used to make floors in the eighteenth century. In the

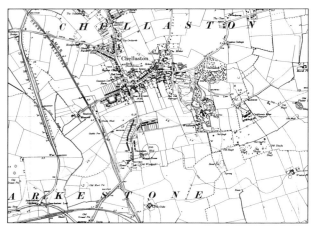

Opposite page: The Forman family were very prominent in Chellaston (and Derby for that matter, where Robert Forman served as Mayor in 1848 and his son Thomas in 1868). Henry (1848-1914) lived at the Yews and was an important figure at the turn of the century. John Forman was his cousin as well as a cousin of Alderman Thomas, and kept the village grocery in the High Street at Chellaston. Here is his wife and a grandchild, with the child's mother standing at the door of the recently rebuilt shop. A vernacular thatched building of c.1800, it was tiled, given new windows and a coat of stucco on the ground floor (grooved to resemble ashlared stonework) a few years before the photograph was taken c.1905. Courtesy the late Cllr Ken Brown. L4461

Some time around 1920, a local resident ascended to the tower of St Peter's church and took a photograph for each half turn. This view is due east, with Green Avenue punctuating the burial ground on this side. Upper left is Whitehouse Farm with Pit Close Farm to the far right. The cottages left of centre on Green Avenue were replacements – put up just before World War One on a line of very ancient thatched ones, and built on the same foundations. Courtesy the late Cllr Ken Brown. L2140

nineteenth century mining and carving it was a major industry in the village. A board school (the building still extant) was erected in 1878. Such industry, combined with the lack of a single great landowner, allowed Chellaston to expand piece-meal. A Methodist chapel was built to serve the increasing working population in 1875, seven years after the completion of a Baptist one. The village also boasted a notable brickworks, and until 1802 when it was enclosed, also sported a triple open field system with four course rotation. For a while, from the mid-nineteenth century, the village had the benefit of a railway station on the Derby-Melbourne line, but by the mid-1930s the passenger service had been withdrawn and communications were by motorbus. Before the railway, the normal conveyance to Derby was by canal boat, especially on market day.

Derby absorbed Chellaston in 1968, and since that date, the village has had its housing stock expanded enormously, a process which yet continues. The transformation from populous village into sizable suburb has been accomplished within 30 years, but at a considerable aesthetic cost.

Further reading:

Chellaston History Group,	*A Chellaston Walk About* (Derby, 1992)
Craven, M. & Stanley, M.	*Derbyshire Country House*, Vol.II (Matlock 1984) 25
Young, J.A.	*Alabaster*, (Matlock 1990)
Young, J.A.	*An Introduction to the History of Chellaston and its Church*, 2nd Ed. (Derby 1983)

Cottons

Name: 'The farm of Codda' – Saxon, mutated from Codinton

COTTON'S Farm marks the site of a deserted medieval village (DMV); the only one known for certain within the City boundary. At the time of the Domesday Book it was known as Codinton and had been held by the eponymous Osmond of Osmaston as a separate manor with four bovates. The mutant form of the name Cotton's appeared as early as 1357 (Cameron, EPNS. XXIX, *Derbyshire* (1952) III, 649), and this

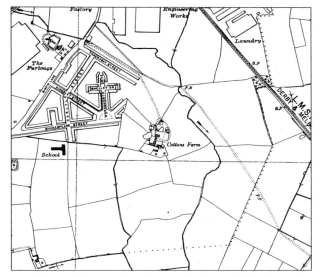

part was one of the hundred-plus manorial holdings of Henry de Ferrers by 1086 (DB.6.89).

Another part of the settlement, also of four bovates, was held under the King as an outlier of the manor of Melbourne by the Bishops of Carlisle. The settlement was within the parish of St Peter, Derby and as such was originally esteemed a portion of the Borough.

By 1156 Codinton was held by Sir Robert de Codinton (Darley Charter A12) and descended to Engenulph de Codinton – the forename suggests Viking ancestry – whose heiress carried the estate to Godfrey de Dethick of Dethick, shortly before 1300. It is clear from Charter evidence that this holding – still four bovates – was assigned to the Canons of the Abbey of St Mary, Darley Abbey about this time by Geoffrey's undertenant, Hugh de Gurney (Darley Charters A58, F4). The fields of Codington were divided into strips and headlands – the classic early medieval three-field system with evenly distributed holdings for the villagers – and charters of *c*.1220 and *c*.1250 mention them (Darley Charters F87, G42). Traces of the medieval ridge and furrow can still be seen at Cottons.

After 1357 charter evidence trails off and it is possible that the village was depopulated to a non-viable level of inhabitants by the Black Death. In the century following the few mentions of it suggest only a croft or two survived and by 1545 it had been absorbed, administratively, by Normanton-by-Derby, also a township within St Peter's Parish. This process was facilitated because the heiress of Dethick transmitted Cottons a junior branch of the Babingtons which had acquired the Lordship of Normanton, and managed to obtain a settlement of the manor of Cottons to consolidate the estate. When the Babingtons sold their land to the Beaumonts of Gracedieu, Leicestershire, *c*.1586 some 285 acres of Cottons were detached by purchase as a freehold farm.

The Shakespeare Street estate, built on Sinfin Lane in the late 1920s and early 1930s probably straddles the site of the deserted Medieval village of Codington. Cottons Farm, the only surviving site is off the view, lower right. The estate's streets are all named after English men of letters – most large towns have an estate so named! The aerial view was taken for Derby County Borough Council *c*.1934. At the top of the picture, is the Austin estate, Normanton.

By the later seventeenth century the land at Cottons was owned and farmed by the Radfords, and it was Edwin Radford (1840-1928) who sold the freehold when he moved to Haynford Lodge, Norfolk around 1920. The purchaser was Derby Corporation, who let the farm as a tenanted small holding, adapting most of the remainder of the estate as Derby's first municipal golf course, opened in torrential rain on 4 July 1923. The rest went for council houses nearby.

Further Reading:

Craven, M.   *Illustrated History of Derby* (Breedon 1988) 44, 183

Woolley W.   *History of Derby* (DRS VI for 1981) 203.

(See also under Normanton.)

Crewton

Name: From the Harpur-Crewe family, who owned the land.

The north side of Baker Street basks in the summer heat, 1955. The neat ordered decorative brick semi-detached artisans' cottages were erected 1907-09. The street was named (as was nearby Chambers Street) after Alderman Robert Baker Chambers (1850-1929), Mayor the year it was pitched: 1906-07. Hall Street was named after the good Alderman's Leicestershire-born mother.

Naturally, Crewton had to have some pubs to quench its residents' thirst, although it has to be admitted that it took more than 30 years before this one was built: The Coronation. This one was planned in 1937 – hence the name: it was the year of George VI's Coronation – but not completed until 1939, again, in Baker Street. Photograph taken by Hurst and Wallace, February 1952. L7737

THIS suburb was originally called (for obvious reasons) Newtown and was carved out of the Northern part of Alvaston parish on land owned by the (Harpur-) Crewe family. This was accomplished in 1901 when a boundary alteration made it part of Derby. The settlement was founded around 1880, occupying the land on either side of London Road south-east of the canal and north of the old Parliamentary boundary. A board school was built in 1890 (with accommodation for 300 children) and a mission church was built the following year at the expense of the wife of Alderman W.B.Robotham. The Congregat-

Where exactly Crewton shades off into Alvaston has ever been a grey area, yet Alvaston Library (set in Alvaston Park) on London Road was undoubtedly in Crewton. One of two Derby Libraries founded in 1913 by the Carnegie United Kingdom Trust, it was designed by Arthur Eaton (1857-1940), completed in 1916, but not opened (through 'lack of resources' – a familiar enough mantra today!) until 1 January 1920. It was made redundant in the early 1970s and demolished after some years as the museums' store, in 1978. Photograph taken in 1936. L1760

ionalists also erected a chapel at this period, along with the Methodist New Connexion.

Regarding transport, all relevant information will be found under Alvaston, although when the trolley buses began a turning loop was put in at Brighton Road, Crewton, so certain services could be terminated there.

Because of its restrictive size and because it was largely built up before World War One, little further development has occurred in the suburb.

Further reading:

Craven, M.   *Illustrated History of Derby* (Breedon, 1988) 215, 220

Darley Abbey

Name: 'Wild animal (or deer) clearing' (= Anglo Saxon, *deor, leah*).

I N 1086 this place, about a mile north of the town, was undoubtedly an unsettled outlying portion of Derby. In 1146, however, the canons of St Helen's, Derby (established by a burgess called Towy in 1137) had outgrown their quarters in the town and needed to move, although finding a site was a problem. Within two years Hugh de Derby, Dean of Derby (a close kinsman of the Touchets of Markeaton and a

Before Strutt's Park was built over in the 1890s, parkland, all created by William Emes, a local disciple of 'Capability' Brown, stretched from St Helen's to Darley Hall. In 1821 a central chunk of it, fronting the upper Duffield Road, was appropriated for a third large house, Mr Thomas Bridgett's Darley Grove built that year to a design of Alderman Richard Leaper (1756-1838). This is Richard Keene's view in this part of the park – by this time renamed Derwent Bank and owned by W.H.Worthington – taken in the 1870s looking south-west. The path still exists. L484

Only a few yards north of Derwent Bank the Arterial Road was laid out connecting Duffield Road with Kedleston Road. This was Broadway, pitched through Mr Richardson's parkland of The Leylands in 1931. This view, looking down towards the small roundabout on Kedleston Road and Markeaton Park Lake beyond was taken in the 1950s. Since then the coming of the A38 extension has savaged this corner of the park, although it has at least turned Broadway into a bosky backwater.

Right: Darley Park was landscaped in 1778 by William Emes of Bowbridge Fields, Mackworth, whilst Pickford was rebuilding the fine house for Robert Holden. This few, taken in January 1903, shows part of the park from across the Derwent. It became a public park in 1929 when the last owner, Mrs Adelaide Evans left it and the house to the town in her will. L1336

member of a Norse family) gave all his family lands at Little Darley (sic) for the purpose, which led to the foundation of the Abbey of St Mary, Darley, Derbyshire's largest monastery, under Albinus, the first Abbot. Robert de Ferrers, Earl of Derby, was patron, the Crown taking over that role after the fall of the Ferrers family in 1268.

The accumulation of residences of lay persons who serviced the new monastery must have laid the basis for the subsequent village, although the whereabouts of the main monastic buildings and church are still obscure. Most guesses centre on the site of the later hall, with ancillary buildings scattered to the north, like the splendid thirteenth-century hall which survived as tenements and is now the Abbey Inn.

The monastery was finally dissolved in 1538 whereupon Robert Sacheverell acquired the site, and asset-stripped it before selling on to Sir William West, who probably adapted the former Abbot's lodging as a capital mansion (as happened elsewhere in England) – hence the reasonable belief that the Abbey buildings must have underlain the site of the later hall, erected to a design by Francis Smith of Warwick in 1727 for Alderman William Woolley, son of the county's historian. The park stretched then to the north side of Bridge

A postcard of Darley Park and the Hall of 1952, after its municipalisation. The uniformed children are there because the hall was then Central School. When it moved to a new building on Breadsall Hill Top in 1961 (and was renamed Henry Cavendish after the great eighteenth century Chatsworth-born chemist) the hall was summarily destroyed despite a grade II listing – a tragedy.

Gate and on the west to the crest of the hill, up which runs Duffield Road, created by turnpiking in 1756. The course of the ancient trackway which preceded it can still be seen crossing Darley Park to this day. In 1767 the park of St Helen's was carved out of it and in 1821 that of Derwent Bank.

In 1778 Robert Holden, having acquired the house and estate, had the former rebuilt by Joseph Pickford of Derby and the park landscaped by that able local follower of Capability Brown, William Emes, producing the stunning natural *coup de l'oeuil* we can see today.

One thing which may have existed at Darley from the days of the Abbey was a mill. In the 1770s there was a paper mill and a water-powered flint mill. When the crooked banker John Heath went bust in March 1779, he owned both and, by a strange coincidence, the receiver in bankruptcy – Derby financier Thomas Evans – managed to acquire both very cheaply! The flint mill he quickly rebuilt (possibly with Pickford's help) as an advanced cotton mill 1781-82, rebuilding and adding more after a fire a few years later. The mill was locked into the transport network by an arm of the canal from the mill weir to St Mary's Bridge.

Walter Evans (1764-1839) built a fine new house called Darley House (perhaps designed

Between Broadway and where St Ralph Sherwin School now stands Duffield Road passes through a locality and by a farm (long demolished) called Mile Ash, connected to Darley Abbey village by a surviving lane. This view dates from *c*.1904 and was taken by F.W.Scarratt of Derby.

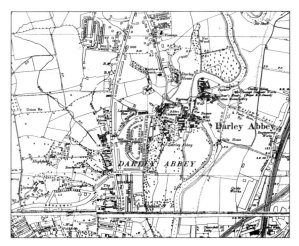

Not much further along from where the previous view was taken, was this one, but looking south, instead of north. Mile Ash farm's roof is just visible to the right, and the village is beyond and much below the trees, left. Photo taken by Hurst & Wallis, 1924 as part of a bus route survey.

by his talented brother-in-law, William Strutt FRS) about 1790, but in 1844 the Evanses moved to Darley Hall. The village was built up to a high standard from 1782 to about 1825 by the Evanses for their workforce, and church and school (the former at least designed by Moses Wood of Nottingham) were added in 1819. It now forms, with the mill, as fine a 'model' village of the Regency period as can be found anywhere in the UK. It is marred by the loss of the Hall (demolished by the council, 1962) and Darley House (demolished by a developer in 1934) and the concomitant spread of rather ordinary houses over the park of the latter and part of the estate of the former, mainly in the 1960s and 1970s. The mill closed in the late 1960s but still flourishes after a fashion, split up into small industrial units. The sale of another estate on the west side of Duffield Road, has led to further building there, centred on Broadway, the local segment of the 1930s Ring Road.

A final piece of parkland was preserved by the building of Highfields for Henry Evans, a younger son, in the 1880s. This later became St Philomena's Convent, which preserved the house and mature wooded park. Unfortunately the Nuns have recently (1995) sold this to a developer who plans to build extensively on the parkland to the enormous detriment of the suburb.

The Evans family transformed Darley Abbey between 1782 and about 1840. Quite apart from the commodiousness and simple dignity of the surviving artisans' cottages, they provided excellent community buildings. This is one of them, the school, an elegantly proportioned and finely detailed classical building erected in 1826. The central floating pediment with its Whitehurst & Son clock is bold, as are the windows set in the blind arcade. The architect is unknown, unfortunately; it cost Walter Evans £3,000, so it was by no means cheap! L8419

The two world wars both led to the creation of part-time military units dedicated to the defence of their local community. *Dad's Army* has made us all familiar with the World War Two version, but this postcard of 1916 shows World War One Darley Abbey home guard unit (drawn exclusively from Mrs Evans' employees, needless to say) posed for Mr F.W.Scarratt's camera. The unit comprised boys too young to go to the front, men too old, partly disabled people and those in protected occupations. L 6977

A view in Darley Street showing the decorations and festivities laid on by Mrs Evans to assist the villagers in celebrating George V's Coronation in 1911. There were two green arches labelled 'G R' – for Georgius Rex – and 'M R' – for Maria Regina: King George and Queen Mary. L2523

The oldest and most celebrated building in Darley village is without doubt the Abbey Inn. This was felicitously converted into a pub by Richard Wood in 1979. The building, then long derelict, but previously converted by the Evans family as workers' cottages, is the only authentic surviving part of the former Abbey of St Mary, Darley, once Derbyshire's largest monastery. It would appear to date from *c*.1300 and later, but its original function and relationship to the rest of the Abbey is not known. Richard Keene took the photograph *c*.1889. All the houses survive, but have been somewhat spoilt by inappropriate windows and lavish applications of white paint and snowcem.

Further reading:

Craven, M. & Stanley, M.	*The Derbyshire Country House* (Breedon 1991) 65-69
Craven, M.	*The Derby Town House* (Breedon 1987) 107, 109-111
Darlington, R.R.	*The Cartulary of Darley Abbey* DRS.1. (Kendal, 1945) 2 Vols.
Peters, D.	*Darley Abbey* (Hartington, 1974)

An Edwardian view north along Abbey Lane. All the buildings in front of which the group of people are standing still exist, but most of the trees have gone. In the distance, on the corner of Old Lane, is now a recently-closed cycle shop. L11263

A view of the toll house on Duffield Road at the corner of Mile Ash Lane built in the 1850s but made redundant by dis-turnpiking in 1888 and turned into a shop. Demolished to make way for houses before the war. L11260

Dunkirk, Kensington and St Luke's

Name: From the French port, first recorded by P.P.Burdett's map (1767) but conceivably going back to the time of Queen Mary I's loss of that place.

THE land lying between the Odd Brook, later Uttoxeter New Road, and Burton Road was long known as Abbey Barns, being a portion of a larger medieval arable area called the Newlands which had at an early stage been given to the Abbey of Darley. Dunkirk was almost certainly a small farm of post-reformation date, and lay immediately to the north of Abbey Barns, a small community consisting of a couple of smallholdings and another farm.

The first developments in the area were Little City (qv.) and Kensington. The latter

A view northwards down Kensington Street towards Curzon Street, before this thoroughfare was shortened, summer 1962. The cottages on the left were all built by John Harpur (1781-1851) – interestingly a descendant of Sir John Harpur of Calke, 1st Bt. – part-owner of the Rowditch Brickworks in the 1820s. He lived in Talbot Street. L11235.

Parallel with Kensington Street was Talbot Street which debouches into Curzon Street precisely where that thoroughfare becomes Uttoxeter New Road and where, later, Stafford Street was pitched, defining the south-east boundary of the Great Northern Railway's Friar Gate station and goods yard complex, built 1876 and clearly visible in this 1962 photograph. L11228

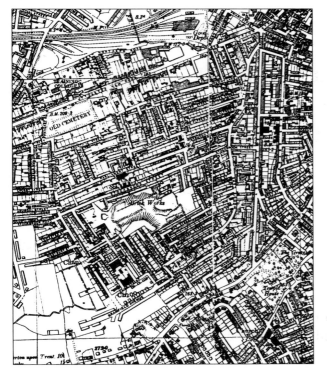

consisted of two streets (Talbot and Kensington Streets) running between Dayson Lane (later Curzon Street) and Drewry Lane, developed c.1810 by the Drewrys (proprietors of the *Derby Mercury*) and the Harpurs (Rowditch Brickmakers) on land acquired from Lord Scarsdale. In the mid-1840s Drewry Lane and Dunkirk were developed and much of the north-east end of Abbey Street was built in the 1830s. West of Dunkirk was a large brickyard, in the hands of the Du Sautoy family, but the area surrounding it gradually began to be developed with a mixture of narrow tapes mills and artisans' cottages from the mid-1850s for about two decades. In 1868-1871 Josias Frederick Robinson built a new church there dedicated to St Luke, the parish being carved out of that of St Werburgh. The widow of Alderman Moss was the patron.

Since the later 1960s much of the area

Three views of the common yard at the Dunkirk end of Drewry Lane. Each house had a privy, with its number on it, and there are fourteen altogether bearing the numbers of houses in Kensington Street. The houses do not appear to have been altered since Mr Harpur built them one hundred and thirty years earlier; they have definitely declined into slums. Photographs taken in the 1950s, shortly before clearance. L11231.

Talbot Street again, taken on the same day as the previous view, but facing the other way, with the photographer with his back to Curzon Street. In the distance is Drewry Lane; left, a rather nice Mark 1 Vauxhall Victor. L11235

Corner shops abounded, and where there was not a corner shop there was a pub. This is the Talbot Street/Drewry Lane east corner showing Mrs Newbold's shop in 1962-typical of its kind but today a great rarity. L11029 & 11786

has been pulled down, and the housing stock largely replaced, although quite a bit of Dunkirk itself and Drewry Lane have survived along with much later housing erected on the estate of a large Regency Villa on Burton Road – The Firs – from the 1890s. The brickyard was also filled in, and this area converted into a rather featureless public open space.

A view westwards up Stockbrook Street – not so much Dunkirk as St Luke's, an area represented in notably few photographs – of 21 July 1948. At the extreme left (on the corner of St Luke's Street) is the Parliament House Inn, started around 1867-68. The mill beyond the corner shop was once that of Richard Cooper the Ashbourne corset manufacturer although was built in 1860s for Henry Jackson an elastic web maker, and the distinctive tower of St Luke's church built in 1871 can be seen beyond, over the rooftops. Today, everything except the church has gone, to be replaced by modern (but equally small) houses, extending south beyond St Luke's Street over the site of the former brickworks of Edward du Sautoy. L5603

A view westward up Drewry Lane from Dunkirk. Talbot Street with Mrs Newbold's shop on the corner is clearly visible in the middle distance. Beyond are the premises of James Smith & Son, uniform manufacturers established in 1835 and closed in 1986. Photograph of 1962. L11226

The Monk Street/Dunkirk corner in 1955. Note an enduring Derby institution: Alf James' joke shop, later of Green Lane, and still going, forty years later. L9769

Further reading:
Craven, M.   *Illustrated History of Derby* (Breedon 1988) 136
Payne, C.J.   *Derby Churches Old and New* (Derby 1893) 95-100

Litchurch

Name: Anglo-Saxon, 'Luda's Church' (1086)

N THE Domesday book Litchurch consists of one manor, by then part of the Borough of Derby, although the relevant passage is considered to be an afterthought. The question is: What was Luda's Church? Most commentators consider that St Peter's, Derby may well have been one and the same, absorbed

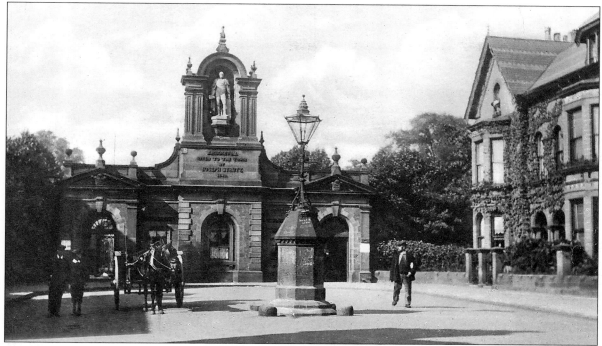

This German-produced postcard of *c.*1904 shows Henry Duesbury's elegant lodge, the lamp and Humphrey's stolid yellow brick houses. Where, in the view below, from the rear of the Lodge there is a clock, on this side stands a statue of the park's donor, Joseph Strutt. The end house on the right was the residence of Joseph Brighouse (1840-1929) for many years organist of St Michael's, and later of Spondon. After decades of dereliction and vandalism, the lodge, built 1850 was refurbished as photographic studios in 1993-94 by the Derbyshire Historic Buildings Trust with inspired help from Derby City Council. L9109

by the southward expansion of the town before 1086. If so, this must, with Wardwick and (possibly) Morledge (which are too central to qualify for this book) be one of the most ancient suburbs. In extent it must have been co-terminous with St Peter's parish less its outliers of Boulton, Normanton, Osmaston and Cottons. It must also have been of some importance before 1066, for it gave its name to the Hundred of Morleston and

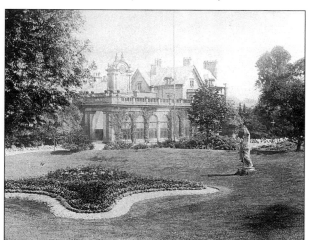

By the 1830s Derby's expansion had outstripped the capacity of its infrastructure – its roads, water supply, sewage, housing, etc. – and the quality of life for all classes was in sharp decline. The gift to the town of the Arboretum, arguably England's first public park, by Joseph Strutt (1765-1844) made a significant contribution towards the reversal of that process. This photograph, taken by Richard Keene in the early 1870s shows the back of the Lodge – which formed an Orangery – with its Whitehurst clock, J.C.Loudon's landscaping and some of the houses of Arboretum Square, designed and built by C.E.Humphreys (1819-1879) in the previous decade. L9632

Apart from Loudon's landscaping, the Arboretum was embellished with urns and statues from Strutt's garden at his home, Thorntree House, St Peter's Street. Other items were acquired later, like the fountain in this 1930s view cast in Derby by Andrew Handyside & Co., Britannia Foundry, Duke Street, but later (as here) shortened. The statue of Sir Henry Royce, Bt. by Derwent Wood RA had been then recently added; later it was moved to the Riverside Gardens and is now outside Rolls-Royce's HQ. The gazebo-like building in the background were designed by E.B.Lamb and built in 1840-41. L11959

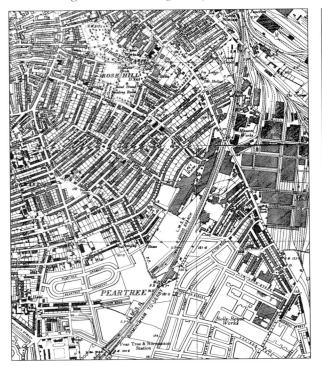

The Handyside fountain in the Arboretum appears in the distance in this view taken from the Rose Hill end (another small suburb bordering the Arboretum's 11 acres). The urns in the foreground also came from Handyside's foundry, being one of their most popular products, smaller copies of the famous Warwick vase. Another pair (but rather larger) stood near the orangery in Markeaton Park, but have inexplicably vanished within the last decade. The ones seen here were probably melted down as part of the 1939-45 war effort. The other urns probably came from Strutt's garden, as did the famous boar.

London Road formed a sort of axis through Litchurch, and the area north of Bradshaw Street might be looked on as its northern boundary. This 1948 view shows the Bradshaw Street/Traffic Street junction in summer 1948, long before the present traffic island was installed. The Granville Hotel was a long-established temperance hotel in a building of c.1800-1810. The author was recently assured that King Edward VII had stayed there anonymously as Prince of Wales with Mrs Langtry. It was the fact that it was a *temperance* establishment (run by the anonymous-sounding Mrs Smith in 1891) which finally made the tale ring false! L5518

from ?

A view down Wellington Street towards the junction with Park Street about 1970. The latter was so named because when it was pitched c.1837-40 it bisected the parkland of Castlefields (demolished 1837) running along the ha-ha. Left, the distinctive tall outline of the admirable Sir Robert Peel Inn, opened December 1938. Despite having had only two landlords since opening it has recently been gutted. The last, the late Alfred Whitehurst (1923-1994) was host from 1953 until his death. He was almost certainly a descendant of James, a brother of John Whitehurst FRS (1713-1788) the eminent Derby horologist. To the right in this scene is part of the large Bemrose complex, demolished in winter 1994-95 to make way, inevitably, for a car park.

Litchurch, formed in the century before. Around 1700 it was a 'liberty of itself but no house, only three or four cottages.'

As Hugh de Derby, the Dean (see Darley Abbey) was the hereditary patron of St Peter's Church, it may be that he was a descendant of its founder, the eponymous Luda; the enigmatic patron of Domesday Book, Edric son of Coln, may therefore stand between them. The church was, however, given by Hugh's family to Darley Abbey, whilst the manorial estate was joined to the extensive holdings of Peter de Sandiacre as a consequence of some 'rationalisation' which took place as a consequence of the town's new Charter of 1203. This seems to have effectively removed Litchurch from Derby, a situation which endured for the following 674 years!

From three households in 1700, Litchurch had barely grown in 1800, yet in 1877 the population stood at 69,716! This was due to the expansion of the town which was made possible by the sale of the Castlefields estate (1803-1856) and parts of the Osmaston Hall estate. Railway installations and foundries (the latter clustered along Cottons Lane) expanded fast and workers' housing was required for them. This led to the township being constituted under a local board in 1860 whereby it became self-governing. As many of Derby's most important citizens lived in the rather fine early Victorian suburb which grew up alongside the Osmaston Road (just as most of Derby's artisans and workers also lived

Litchurch being a very old suburb – what today would be called 'Inner City' – it had a bewildering variety of housing. This poor dilapidated pile was once one of Derby's finest Regency villas. It was called The Field and stood nearly opposite the end of Reginald Street, having been built – it would now seem – around 1800, and perhaps designed by George Moneypenny the younger, although for whom is by no means clear. It had a very chequered history after being sold by Councillor G.E.Franklin around 1914. In this photograph of the late 1960s it lies derelict, after many years as the Fire Service HQ. It was demolished in 1972. The building on the right was a billiard room added *c.*1878 by Alderman Sir Abraham Woodiwiss. L4997

there, too) they worked very hard at improving Litchurch, which had a flying start with the Arboretum in 1840. When a Local Government Reform Act reintegrated Litchurch into Derby in 1877 they fought like tigers to maintain their independence.

Thanks to industry's presence, all modern conveniences came to Litchurch: tramways (1880), new schools, churches and chapels in profusion. The housing stock ranged from 1820s to 1880s in date generally, and much has been renewed in recent years. A greatly lamented loss, however, has been the destruction of Reginald Street Baths (by John Ward, 1904) in the 1980s. Built as a sop to the disgruntled Litchurch magnates, they were never more needed than when closed, the area having declined considerably by then.

The final consideration: the extent of modern Litchurch, taking it as co-terminous with the old local board area, is:

The northern boundary of The Field was marked by Bloomfield Street which ran down to London Road, being crossed about half way along by Barrow Street. This view of January 1957 was taken from the latter of the shop at 59 Bloomfield Street, a newsagents run 20 years before by Mrs Bagnall and later by Violet Wileman. The buildings here would appear to date back to the 1870s. Bloomfield Street was ultimately cleared – for what? one might ask – in the early 1970s.

From the Derwent, across the Siddalls (railway works), railway station (north side), north of Wellington Street and Litchurch Street, along Grove Street, Normanton Road by Lyndhurst Street, then round Industrial, Provident, Co-operative Streets and Lower Dale Road to Pear Tree Road, along Walbrook Road, St Thomas' Road and along a line from the corner of Balfour Road to the top of Elton Road, then along the latter, Cotton Lane, then in a line across to Deadman's Lane and along that to the Derwent again.

Nevertheless, New Normanton (qv.) took a few chunks out of this convoluted boundary in the years following the re-absorption of Litchurch by Derby.

Further Reading:

Craven, M.   *Illustrated History of Derby* (Breedon 1988) 20, 34, 40, 115, 139-42, 215.

Payne, C.J.   *Derby Churches Old and New* (Derby 1893) 43-50, 70-73, 80-88.

Clearing the less salubrious inner city properties in Litchurch went on throughout the 1950s to the 1970s. Here, in 1959, are the last few houses in Litchurch Street, at least one still occupied. The thoroughfare, like Bloomfield Street, one of a regular grid connecting Osmaston Road to London Road, formed the south-east boundary of the DRI, and consequently was the first of these streets to vanish as the hospital inexorably expanded. L11214

Two views (above and below) of Liversage Place taken in 1948. Again, early nineteenth-century artisans' cottages, but very inferior ones compared with those in Oxford Street. The street – then very narrow – connected Traffic Street with Trinity Street and ran parallel with London Road, all enclosing property (including the surviving almshouses of 1836) owned by the Liversage Charity. The Charity, Derby's richest, owns many homes, – a notable concentration north of Nottingham Road has recently been made a conservation area – was established 2 August 1529 by Robert Liversage of St Peter's Parish, an opulent dyer, and his childless wife Alice. L5507, L5504

Yet another of these streets was Oxford Street – even before the Mackworth estate came, Derby had always boasted streets with a London sound to them but without the cachet on the ground! This view was also taken in January 1957. The artisans' cottages are much earlier than those in Bloomfield Street and are well proportioned late Regency examples with excellent sash windows and bracket cornices. Note the VW Beetle with early bodyshell parked near what used to be called a shooting brake. All swept away by DRI expansion.

Opposite page: The famous triangle of cottages designed in 1840 by Francis Thompson for the North Midland Railway was preserved just over a decade ago by the joint action of the Derby Civic Society and the Derbyshire Historic Buildings Trust after a prolonged period of decline which this view of Leeds Place, Railway Terrace, epitomises. The photograph was taken 11 November 1953.

Yet Leeds Place was no means the worst housing in Litchurch. Off Park Street lay Park Place, where the housing, despite being of the most basic type, managed to survive clearance until the mid-1950s as this 1953 view testifies. Note the still cobbled street and pavement, the high wall of an engineering works and its gantry fixed right up against the dwellings. L5909

A most superior Regency villa – yet smaller and later than The Field – was Litchurch, Villa, built as a town residence by the Bateman family of Hartington Hall *c.*1830, hence Bateman Street (of similar date) defining the south boundary. Just after World War One it was purchased by Rolls-Royce for use as an employees' club and is here depicted early on in the Rolls-Royce era *c.*1923. A bowls tournament is in progress, with the villa's garden front behind and a Bateman Street house visible, left. *Courtesy Rolls Royce Plc.* L12131

A late 1960s view up Clifton Street, yet another of the streets which used to connect London and Osmaston Roads, now truncated by hospital expansion or merely obliterated. This row of seven cottages are exceptionally stylish and were constructed in *c.*1858-60 for the workers at Alderman Henry Fowkes' ironworks in nearby Osmaston Road. Not only did the cottages have cast-iron sills, capitals (of the recessed arcading) and other details usually done in stone, but surprisingly good sized rooms and generous staircases. Until summer 1995 the house with the white door survived thanks to a stubborn occupant; a ruinous house survived on either side. L10889

The Derbyshire Royal Infirmary replaced the old General Infirmary on the same site on London Road in the 1890s. The site was originally part of the Castlefields estate, acquired in 1806. Before the advent of the Health Service, the hospital was run by trustees (heavily influenced by the old Borough Council) and each summer Hospital Day was held to raise money for the institution. It was an event much enjoyed by all levels of Derby society and involved fancy dress, eccentric activities, parties and other fun activities. In 1921 the week ('day' was a misnomer) culminated on 29 June with a visit by King George V and Queen Mary who were guests of honour at a garden party in the Infirmary Grounds. In this view the Royal arrival is eagerly anticipated. L2647

There is a well-known and much published photograph of the Litchurch Fire Brigade in the 1870s when it was an independent body. This view shows the Litchurch station crew outside their depot in Bloomfield Street in the 1930s when they were firmly part of the Derby County Borough Fire Brigade, coming under the control of Capt. Rawlings, the Borough's chief constable. L1077

Little Chester

Name: Roman *Derventio* (from the old British *Deru Wen* river name = Derwent, 'abounding in oaks' from the seventh century *Ravenna Cosmography*, being a copy of a Roman original). 1086 Cestre, Old English = fortification, 1232 *Parva Castra* (Little fortification), rendered first in English 1369.

FOUNDED in the later first century by the Romans, the supposed military role of this vital river-crossing settlement quickly was lost as a prosperous small town grew up, latterly partly behind very considerable stone walls. Commercial activity appears to have ceased by the beginning of the fifth century, although it is quite unclear for how long the walls remained a place of refuge for

As Derby's oldest suburb and the focus of its Roman predecessor, some of its thoroughfares are also almost 2,000 years old. This view of City Road emphasises its straightness, running as it does from St Mary's Bridge to the approximate centre of the Roman settlement where it crosses Old Chester Road at a right angle. It is to be presumed that, within the Roman walls, these formed the *cardus* and *decumanus* (main axes) of the ancient town of *Derventio*. This view of *c.*1965 is a view north showing the Great Northern Railway Bridge (removed 1967), Bliss' factory (originally Sir Alfred Haslam's Union foundry of 1867) on the left and the medieval common of Chester Green on the right. L2205/28

the native Romano-British population. Eventually the settlement was probably abandoned for a time.

In the sixth century the English arrived but it is not known if a new community then sprang up as part of the wide area called by then Northworthy. Either way, it was certainly refortified after 874 by the Norsemen and it was from there that Queen Aethelflaeda ejected them, four of the thegns being 'killed within the gates' in 917 (or 921). The Vikings, we think, coined the name Derby (Deoraby) (= 'Der(went) Place') from that of the old Roman fort, which was later transferred to Derby when the Saxon *burh* was founded a few years later, and the older settlement was granted by the King to the newly-founded Royal Free Chapel of All Saints' Derby as endowment, with Little Eaton (qv.). Thereafter it seems most likely that a small village grew up to become Little Chester.

All Saints' was a Collegiate Minster church, that is, there were six canons and a Dean (later a sub-dean) who were supported by the income of one each of seven farms which by then comprised the community of Little Chester. At the Dissolution of the College, 1548-49, these became the property of the Borough and were let. Other land at Little Chester had long been let to lay people, like the mill, boat yard, etc. Some common land lay within the township, too.

It was not until the late eighteenth

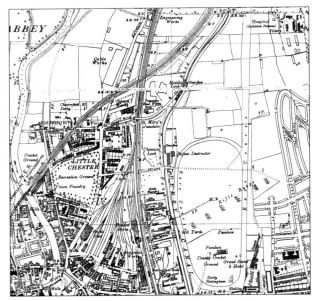

Mansfield Road is not Roman, but is a late route from St Mary's Bridge northwards, only approximating to the Roman alignment. This view to the south shows the Duke of Clarence Inn *c.*1957. The Regency appearance of the building – actually two artisan's cottages run together – would confirm the first listed date for the inn as 1827. It was named after George III's third son, so created 1789 who succeeded to the throne as William IV in 1830. The cars are a pre-war Rover and a (then) newish Vauxhall Velox. L4554

century that things began to change. The Borough was short of money and began to sell land. One plot, by the Derwent, just north of St Mary's Bridge, was sold to Thomas Gisborne of St Helen's House, who let it to his ex-footman, James Fox, to build a precision engineering works, and before long several other foundries like Cheetham & Hill, as well as other industries, e.g. colour making, became established there. Further, in the 1860s,

The City Tavern was built on the largely defunct Roman road which ran east from *Derventio* to Sawley ferry, the extant stub-end of which was later named Vivian Street, the remainder of it having been submerged underneath the Midland Railway line from 1840. The inn was built in 1850 by a local baker, John Thornhill and was a bakery and draper's shop before becoming a tavern. Locals used to bring their Sunday joints for cooking in the bakehouse oven, and Thornhill instituted a type of local 'co-op' wherein the customers could obtain a dividend purchases of bakery items. It became an inn by 1878, having been painted (as here, looking west down Vivian Street) *c.*1870, when still a shop. Purchased in the 1920s by Home Ales who replaced it with a new building called the Garden City, doubtless after Welwyn, then newly established. (Courtesy late C.H.Burton, L269)

the Midland Railway bought a large tract of land on the east of Mansfield Road to build a large complex of sidings and warehouses. The population, meanwhile, had risen from a hundred or so to over five hundred by 1850 when a new Anglican church – St Paul's Chester Green – was built to designs by Barry & Brown, joining a handful of nonconformist chapels already in place.

In 1867 one of the foundries – Haslam's – specialising in refrigeration equipment, absorbed Fox's to produce the huge Union Foundry (today E.W.Bliss & Co) on City Road and over the next forty years Sir Alfred Haslam built large numbers of good houses for his workforce, some set around the Green, itself created a public park in the 1880s.

In 1876 the Great Northern Railway Ilkeston to Derby (Friar Gate) line was commenced and this sliced through the north and western parts of the suburb until 1968 when the high

In 1719 William Stukeley drew a map of Little Chester, and this clearly shows the Coach and Horses (then called the Crown) on the corner of Mansfield Road and Old Chester Road. It had acquired its present title by 1750 when coaches may have started using it. In 1871 Alderman Clarke's brewery owned it, and in 1905 it became the property of Offiler's who rebuilt it approximately as seen in this photograph of February 1952, looking up the Roman alignment of Old Chester Road towards the second of Little Chester's vanished railway bridges. L7694

One of the three prebendal farms surviving World War Two at Little Chester (or four, if Little Chester House, now part of Richard Daniel's works marks the site of one) was the Manor House, an early seventeenth-century brick building of great charm, built directly on to the foundations of a Roman building excavated in 1988. Unfortunately the grade III listed building was demolished in 1964, and a garage erected on the site, itself since replaced (1989) by houses. This view shows the rear of the Manor (the south front) lying derelict, June 1963. L3896

embankment was removed and extensive excavations of the Roman remains sealed beneath it were undertaken.

Little Chester, which includes Derby racecourse and all the land up to Beaufort Street and Old Mansfield Road in the east, Nottingham Road in the south, the Derwent on the west and Darley and Little Eaton in the north, continues to flourish and became a conservation area in 1993.

Further reading:

Burton, C.H.   *Little Chester* (Derby 1989)

Craven, M.   *Illustrated History of Derby* (Breedon 1988) 9-31

Langley, R.S. & Drage C.   *Roman Occupation at Little Chester, Derby* (Derby, 1990)

Dool J., Wheeler, H., *et al Roman Derby, Excavations 1968-1983*, in Derbyshire Archaeological Journal CV (1985) *passim*

Paxton, E.A.   *The Church of St Paul, Derby* (Derby 1950) – pageant programme

Old Chester Road ends at the eastern bank of the Derwent. Facing each other on either side of that part of the road west of City Road are the two surviving Prebendal Farms. In this view from the Derwent facing east of c.1878, the newly-erected GNR bridge over the street (visible from the other side in the view of the Coach and Horses) can be seen in the distance, whilst to the left is Derwent House and far right, some outbuildings relating to the main prebendal farm, Stone House Prebend. (Courtesy Mr & Mrs P.Haslam.) L5905

Little Chester is often incorrectly referred to as Chester Green, although the latter is merely the large open feature on the west side of Mansfield Road bounded by St Paul's Road, City Road and Chester Green Road. It lay south of the Roman town, and although there may be evidence of Roman settlement beneath its turf, it does not mark the site of the ancient city. This view of it was taken from the GN Railway embankment looking down Marcus Street, Spring 1966.

This view is the exact reverse of the previous view taken on the same occasion. Note the smart Triumph Vitesse, right. The housing was erected in the later 1890s, although the Green, for centuries part of the Borough's commons, was opened as a public park in 1886 funded by a sale of land to the Railway Company nine years before. It was originally entirely ringed by an iron fence supported on elegant iron bollards from Abell's foundry. Unfortunately most of these have been hijacked by the City Council for use elsewhere. L2226

Some of the Abell bollards can be seen in this 1954 view across Chester Green northwards from St Paul's Road. Chester Green Road can be seen, left, in the distance, and Mansfield Road through the trees to the right. L831

In the 1860s the Midland Railway built a large cargo trans-shipment complex called St Mary's Wharf between Mansfield Road and their main line. It was bounded on the south by Fox Street – named after the precision instrument manufacturer James Fox (1760-1835) who was set up in Little Chester with the help of Revd Thomas Gisborne of St Helen's, Joseph Wright's friend, in 1785. This view is from its east end, a junction with Clarke Street, itself named after Alderman Thomas Clarke (1814-1877) the brewer whose premises were adjacent. Clarke was also the last owner of the Derby China factory, nearby on Nottingham Road, before its closure in 1848. Photograph taken in 1959.

This view is looking north up the Midland main line at the point where the sidings serving St Mary's Wharf join, controlled by the signal box seen here. The bridge is that of 1840 which carries Mansfield Road over the line from Little Chester towards Breadsall. The City Tavern is out of sight just a few yards to the left!

Little City

Name: Obscure, but probably no older than c.1810-15. Formerly part of a suspected medieval settlement called The Hay recorded first in a charter of c.1240 (*Haeg* = enclosure).

MORE of a locality than a separate suburb, but with its own distinctive characteristics, Little City lay north-west of Burton Road and Green Lane and had its origin in Thomas Madeley's Haarlem Mill of c.1815. All built by 1819 when it appears on Swanwick's and Rogerson's maps. The standard of housing was extremely poor, although the area survived World War Two before being cleared to be replaced by a large car-park and some flats.

The odd thing about Little City was that the pattern of streets and plots bore no relationship whatsoever either to the hedgerows which preceded them or the streets which

Trafalgar Street was one of the four remarkably mean streets which, with part of Burton Road, comprised Little City. This view of three smiling corporation workmen 'tinning up' the empty houses there in 1959 amply demonstrates the poor quality of the housing Mr Madeley provided for his workforce. The name of the street, along with Waterloo Street, adjacent, emphasises the date of construction *c.*1816, only a few months after the end of the war which culminated in the victory over Napoleon I at Waterloo. L11919, 5516

were laid out round them in the years which followed its establishment. All served by an inn, The Tailor's Arms, and a beerhouse, the Dog & Duck.

Further reading:

Craven, M. *Illustrated History of Derby* (Breedon 1988) 136, 137, 148, 156, 190, 204

Even in February 1959, when this view was also taken, some of the houses in Trafalgar Street were still occupied, as this small group of residents testifies. Major and Barnes' Garage on Burton Road is just visible in the distance at the end of Britannia Street. In the middle distance Haarlem Street crosses. L5560

This view of Britannia Street taken from the Haarlem Street/Trafalgar Street junction shows a surviving portion of the mill with Burton Road beyond and the spire of Christ Church, Normanton Road. Much demolition has already taken place, July 1959. L8390

Little City on 2 March 1960 with all the squalor finally cleared. In the distance, the top of Green Lane and the tower of F.W.Waller's Green Lane Art College of 1878, now part of the University. The area became partly rather dreary flats and a large car park, both of which survive. L5848

An aerial view of the south-west side of Derby in the 1930s, showing Babington Lane and Burton Road slicing across the left-hand side of the view, with Abbey Street converging in the middle distance. Also in the middle distance, centre left, are the close-packed roofs of the constricted alleys of Little City, clustered around their not over-large mill.

Little Eaton

Name: *Detton* in 1086, *Eyton* in 1232 and Little Eaton by 1392. Meaning of the Old English: 'the farm by marshy ground between two streams'.

I N 1086 this settlement, largely on low lying land between the Derwent and the Bottle Brook, was, like Little Chester, part of the endowment of the combined College of All Saints' and St Alkmund. The implication of this is that the settlement may have been specifically wrested from the Norse by Aethelflaeda's forces in 917, and thus pertained subsequently directly to the Crown, like Little Chester. Unfortunately little further evidence can be adduced to support this. Little Eaton's command of the narrow defile of the Bottle Brook and the existence, perhaps, of a strong point preceding Horsley Castle may have had something to do with its importance.

The toll booth, Alfreton Road. Because Little Eaton represented the north-east limit of Derby until the 1860s, travellers did not have to pay a toll until they left the village. The late eighteenth-century toll booth is pictured here in a Richard Keene platinotype in 1887 – complete with toll gate posts, lantern and tariff board – less than a year before it finally became redundant with the winding up of the remaining turnpike trusts. (Courtesy Peter Brady, Esq.) L9300

A gentle summer scene from the 1890s: two local boys sit on the parapet of the sluice by Stanley's Mill, Alfreton Road. Part of the mechanism for operating the sluice is clearly visible, left. (Courtesy Peter Brady Esq.)

Crossing the Derwent between Darley Abbey and Duffield was not easy. The only place between the two was Ford Lane Bridge, which carried what was essentially a farm track from Ford Lane, Allestree across the flimsy looking 40 yard long by nine foot wide timber structure, built by a contractor working on Little Eaton waterworks and later sold to Derby Corporation. In the 1930s it was rebuilt in concrete, and the lane now comes out by the Little Chef Restaurant on the Little Eaton (Abbey Hill) roundabout. The original ford had been destroyed by floods. (Courtesy Peter Brady, Esq.).

Although Philip de Willoughby enclosed a park at Little Eaton in the late twelfth century, the land was largely held in chief by the Dean of Lincoln, to whom the College of All Saints' and St Alkmund, Derby, had been given. He enjoyed an income of over £3 per annum from rights of free warren, timber, a quarry, a mill, subletting land and fishing. An extra mill was added by Thomas Stanley in 1489 'above Jack Darleigh Bridge' – the first recorded instance of the name. Until 1813 all ecclesiastical transactions were conducted through the Derby parish church of St Alkmund, the dissolution of the College in Derby in 1548 notwithstanding. There was anciently a Chapel of St Paul at Little Eaton, but by the early eighteenth century was partly ruinous and later on quite unusable and secularised. It was taken down by the vicar of St Alkmund's and replaced by a new, but much smaller building. This was enlarged in 1837 and replaced in feeble neo-Norman style in 1851. It became a parish in 1861; before it had been a perpetual curacy under the patronage of the vicar of St Alkmund. It was at this juncture that Little Eaton's historic

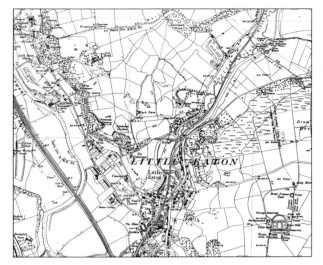

ties with Derby were sundered except for some residual corporate landownership in the new parish. Revd Joseph Pickford was the second perpetual curate of Little Eaton, 1803-1838: the son of the celebrated local architect.

In 1796 the Derby canal arm was opened. Cargoes were trans-shipped at the wharf to a plateway which was built in conjunction with the canal and ran to Denby Bottles. It was usually referred to as the Little Eaton Gangway, and closed in 1908. The Midland Railway also built a branch through the village from the 1840s which, although long closed to passengers, is still open to freight traffic.

The parish was enclosed in 1789 and it was once a great centre of quarrying, paper mills and stocking frames, but is now very much a commuters' village: it has all the disadvantages of a Derby suburb without the administrative benefits and lower Council Tax.

One of many postcard views of Little Eaton. This was taken from the field path above and north-east of the village on the east side of the valley. Jack O'Darley's Bridge is far below and out of sight to the right. Photographed c.1905. (Private collection)

Previous page, top: Another view of part of Little Eaton from Moor Lane, with the valley below through which is concentrated, in a narrow defile, the Bottle Brook, the Ripley branch of the Midland Railway, the Little Eaton tramway, the Old Alfreton Road (clearly visible in this 1956 view) and its successor, the A61. All these elements of communication interweave throughout the length of the village, their routes punctuated by the stone built houses. In this 1956 view, too, one can see the quarry and site of Stanley's Mill. (Courtesy Peter Brady, Esq.) L9261

Bottom: Until the middle of the century there were a surprising number of surviving vernacular buildings of considerable antiquity, quite a few of them timber-framed. These are an example of the latter, timber-framed cruck cottages, their thatched roofs shielded in corrugated iron sheeting, part of Vickers Row situated in Station Road. One cottage still retained its 'pull-up' ladder for access to the upper floor right to the end. The photograph was taken in 1956, about four years before these largely unaltered survivals were swept away, virtually unmourned, to make way for some particularly poorly designed council houses. (Courtesy Peter Brady, Esq.) L9285

Further reading:

Butler, W.O., *et al*
Little Eaton, a Village Surveyed (Belper 1956)

Payne, C.T.
Derby Churches Old and New (Derby 1893) 187-89.

Littleover

Name: 1086: *Parva Oufra* = 'Little ridge' (as opposed to Mickleover, qv.)

PRIOR to 1066, Littleover had, along with its parent manor of Mickleover, been held by the King. By 1086, however, William the Conqueror had granted it at the Abbey of Burton. Nevertheless, a late Norman church had been built (as a Chapel of Mickleover) for the round headed doorcase survives, much moved about, in the fabric of the present church. Most of the medieval church was, however, of fourteenth-century date, but

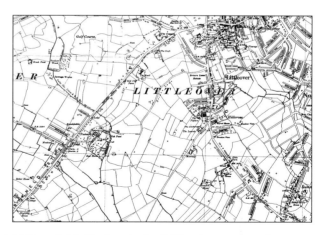

it underwent so many rebuildings between 1857 and 1961 that it is difficult now to discern any real evidence of it. The church is dedicated to St Peter and in 1866 became the centre of a new parish.

The Lordship of Littleover appears to have been let by the Abbey of Burton to the Finderns of Findern; after the Reformation they acquired full title to it, and it came to Sir

A sylvan view taken by Richard Keene of St Peter's Parish church from the south in the 1860s, not long after the medieval building was rebuilt by Henry Isaac Stevens of Derby (1807-1873) in 1857; the newness of the work is still apparent. A very refined Norman doorcase remains in the church and further fragments of Norman decorative work were uncovered during subsequent enlargements of 1908 and 1959-1961. L8372

Richard Harpur of Swarkestone by marriage. Thereafter, until the mid-eighteenth century, Littleover Hall (rebuilt *c*.1600) became the seat of a junior branch of the family, whose heiress ultimately transmitted it to the Heathcotes whose connection ended only after World War One, although they

The interior of the church shortly after the 1908 alterations, which majored on the provision of a new south aisle (R). The east window is Stevens' work, and he also designed the excellent Chellaston alabaster pulpit, carved by Joseph Hall of King Street. Near it can be seen the splendid Renaissance monument to Sir Richard Harpur of Littleover Hall (1635) carved from the same material. Some years ago, liturgical re-ordering' spoiled the chancel and led to the removal of the pulpit, vandalism dictated by fashion.

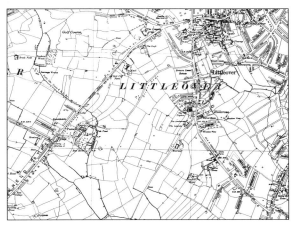

Littleover has a number of large houses, of which by far the most interesting and distinguished is The Pastures, the garden front of which is seen here shortly after rebuilding in *c.*1890. It began as a modest villa *c.*1790, and was rebuilt and extended in 1806 by Richard Leaper (1756-1835) for the Peels, for whom the Queen's gardener, their cousin, Revd Christopher Alderson (1737-1814) laid out the park, seen here in its stunning maturity. (Author. L9370)

forsook the Old Hall (replaced in the 1890s) for The Pastures nearby which they inherited around 1800.

Little expansion affected Littleover until the Derby tramway network was extended as far as the Borough boundary on Burton Road in July 1908. When the trams were replaced by trolley buses in 1933 the route was extended through the village to Chain Lane, the last bus running 3 October 1964 thereafter to be replaced by motor buses.

The Pastures, the walled garden. This was laid out in the 1840s, probably by Lord Harrington's gardener, William Barrow of Breaston (1805-1891). The fine gates were cast by Weatherhead, Glover & Co of Duke Street, Derby. Today most of the park and gardens have been built on by the company Birch plc, including this portion. Forming virtually a new suburb called Heatherton this development is extremely dense and crowds far too closely on what remains of Alderson's fine park; a paradise of plastic fenestration! (Author. L4416)

In 1890 part of the parish was transferred to that of St Werburgh, Derby, which effectively marked the start of the slow process of absorption of Littleover within the city. Its population was then just under 1,000. Enclosure had taken place in 1790.

In 1928 a part of the parish was absorbed by Derby (after a doughty resistance led by Col. Gascoyne) and this enabled the Borough Council to construct the Ring Road (Manor Road and Warwick Avenue) through what had been the northern part of the parish. The remainder followed in 1968, although by this time Littleover had been built up considerably in the 1930s by the sale of land from The Grange and Pastures estates. Much of the arable land of the latter (sold by the

Heathcotes) was acquired by the tenant farmers. It was their descendants' decision to sell up and cash in, in recent years which has enabled the vastly unattractive development south-east of the Burton Road to take place. Part of this bears the distinct modern name of Heatherton, the first syllable of which is supposed to derive from Heathcote.

The end of the lake at The Pastures with the iron bridge of *c.*1890, photographed *c.*1905. It remains – just – but even the lake has been circumscribed by the baleful 'executive homes' that comprise Heatherton. The Pastures was finally extended to designs by Alexander MacPherson for Walter Boden the lace manufacturer *c.*1890, but became a geriatric hospital after the war, then a Nurses' training centre (when, mercifully, it was added to the statutory list) and is now a Grammar School. Although it has secured the future (hopefully) of the house and remaining few acres of park, an opportunity was missed when the planners failed to insist on the reinstatement of the building after various insensitive alterations inflicted upon it in Health Service days. (Author. L4993)

Another house was Littleover Grange, which began as another of Derby's attractive Regency villas in *c.*1814 having been probably built for William Edwards, the Derby solicitor, who left to go to Burton upon Tent to found a pottery in 1832. The next owner enlarged it in Italianate style, and it was purchased by Reuben Eastwood (1833-1877) who is said to have added the *campanile* so that he could smoke after dinner and admire the glow from his foundry (Eastwood and Swingler, Osmaston) in the distance. Sadly he died before it was ready and his widow moved in, being succeeded by three of their daughters, Beatrice (1872-1932), Sarah (1870-1934) and Florence (1869-1938). On the death of the latter, Rolls-Royce purchased it, sold the park to Fryers (who erected Boughton Avenue on it) and added a wing (left, in this view of the 1940s). It was sold to the Derbyshire freemasons in 1972, but was gutted in a disastrous fire on 2 December 1990 in which a museum quality collection of artifacts was destroyed. It was again rebuilt by 1992, however. L9450

Between Littleover Old Hall and The Pastures once stood The Knoll, a pleasant house of *c.*1866 by Henry Isaac Stevens for one of the Hurts. On the death of Mrs Hurt in the mid-1890s it was occupied by the Chief Constable of the County, Capt. Herbert Christian Holland MVO, after which it was acquired by Alderman William Blewrs Robotham (b.1863) a member of an extant dynasty of attorneys in Derby and Mayor of Derby in 1909-10 and 1918-19. It was sold after his death and became partly a housing development site and partly the site of Derby High School for Girls, being demolished when building started in 1956. L3849

Further reading:
Craven, M. & Stanley, M.   *The Derbyshire Country House* Vol.2 (Matlock, 1984) 48
Craven, M. & Stanley, M.   *The Derbyshire Country House* (Breedon, Derby 1991) 128-29
Griffiths, I.   *Littleover, Portrait of a Village* (Breedon, Derby 1990)
Scott, A.B.   *Littleover and its Church* (Derby 1916 & Rev. Edn. Derby 1978)
Wightman J.H. & Sizen G.E.   *St Peter's Church, Littleover* (Derby 1961 & Rev. Edn. 1974)

Leaving Derby on the Burton Road, one used to enter Littleover parish at the top of Littleover Hill; a line a few yards east of Horwood Avenue, (pitched about the time that this part of the village was absorbed by Derby in 1928-29), marks the old parish boundary. In this 1924 view south-west along Burton Road towards the village the entrance to Fairfield House can be seen left, so the photographer was standing virtually on the boundary. Fairfield House, demolished in 1934, was built about 1842 and acquired by George Gascoyne (1815-1895) a rich building contractor from John T.Morley, but became empty on the death of his eldest son – a doughty fighter to protect Littleover from encroachments by Derby – in February 1928. The fact that Derby managed to secure an Act to absorb this part of Littleover within nine months of T.H.Gascoyne's death says much for the effectiveness of his struggle! L2254

One effect of the 1928 boundary extension was to enable a start to be made on the Derby Arterial Road, later the Ring Road. With Fairfield House gone and its land sold, the way was clear to build the Warwick Avenue section completed in 1937 and seen here at night just after World War Two looking uncharacteristically quiet! The turning, right, is Valley Road. L2104

Seen here is the point on the north side of Burton Road where North Street and Wade Street debouch jointly on to the main road. A few yards beyond is the Half Moon Inn, then (1920s) recently rebuilt. Opposite is the drive leading to the Grange. Today, between The Grange and the main road is a large car park and a Kwik Save supermarket.

Beside Kwik Save today is a filling station and then a row of 1960s brick shops set back from the road. These replaced a line of much earlier properties built right up to the road. At the west end of these is Park Lane, so-called originally because it ended amongst the yellow brick estate buildings of The Grange (which partly survive as the Grange Hall and a private house) at the edge of the main house's parkland. This 1950s view shows the end of the street almost as it reaches Burton Road. Then as now it is lined with small brick cottages – one of the few reminders of Littleover's rural past, but today all very bijou and improved. L11989

Littleover, being astride a main road running along a ridge, has always tended to expand in a linear way. Hence the present Methodist Chapel is well to the west of the village centre. Designed by Edward Saunders of T.H.Thorpe & Partners, it was opened in 1958. L11486

Below: At the far west end of the village, close to The Knoll, Chain Lane leaves Burton Road to connect with Uttoxeter Road. This is the junction of the two in 1924. The gates, left, gave access to the golf course which then covered the northern flank of 'Little Ridge' – to give the original meaning of the village's Saxon name. Today this site is a roundabout, with Hillsway built at the right running down to the bottom of The Hollow. In the 1930s, too, King's Drive and contiguous streets, swiftly covered the golf course. (L2255)

Running southwards from Burton Road is Shepherd Street, which becomes Normanton Lane beyond the White Swan. This is a turn-of-the-century postcard view looking down Normanton Lane and showing the artisans' cottages built opposite in the 1890s. Beyond the cottages, and well set back on the left, stood the nineteenth-century Vicarage, now demolished. L8795

An aerial view of Littleover from above The Crest (junction of Chain Lane and Burton Road) looking towards Derby. Hillsway is newly laid out, and the prefabricated houses on Bretton Avenue (left middle distance) are but nearing completion, so the date is probably about 1947-48.

Parallel with Normanton Lane runs The Hollow, an ancient hollow way marking the eastern edge of the Park of the Hall and, with its medieval cottage, a much painted, photographed and appreciated beauty spot in the last century. It is now virtually ruined by a hideous development which was put up in the 1970s approximately to the right of this turn-of-the-century view. L3861

The Hollow, of course, ran into Blagreaves Lane, named after the seventeenth-century parish clerk of All Saints, Derby, George Blagreave (1583-1654) whose family farmed the fields which bore their name in the sixteenth century and beyond. The land between the Littleover end of the lane and the brook to the north-east – an area called Hillcross – was developed with Willson Road from c.1936, and later four or five other streets. This view of c.1951 is of an uncompleted Merridale Road looking down to Willson Avenue, the building of which was held up during the war.

Mackworth

Name: *Macaeworde* (1086), 'The enclosure of Macca' (Old English).

MACKWORTH, with Kniveton and part of Allestree, was a berewick – an outlier – of the manor of Markeaton, and thus, like it, was held at the time of Domesday by Hugh d'Avranches, Earl of Chester, in succession to Siward, Earl of Northumbria who had held it prior to the Norman Conquest. Like Allestree, Colle was the subtenant of Hugh's seneschal and undertenant, Goscelin. If Mackworth had any prior history – and presumably it did, at least back to the unknown era of the eponymous Macca – it had links at least with the Romans, whose secondary road from Little Chester to Chesterton (Staffs) via Rocester ran through Mackworth village; indeed excavations have established that the church of All Saints' – founded in the last years of the twelfth century – actually sits upon its alignment. The oldest part of the church today is the chancel (early fourteenth century), although the nave was built two or three generations later, presumably replacing a Norman original. The aisles, porch and tower were added in the mid-fifteenth century, not long before the Mackworth family, hereditary stewards to the Touchets of Markeaton, Goscelin's descendants – ennobled by the former

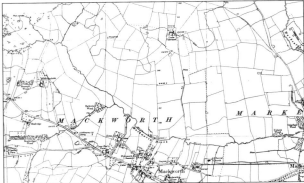

Mackworth church from the south, photographed in 1920. All Saint's church goes back at least to the twelfth century and was built astride Long Lane, the Derby-Rocester Roman Road. Traces were found in an excavation in 1982. The earliest part of the present church is the chancel (c.1325) with the nave dating from the later part of the same century. Most of the remainder is of mid-fifteenth century date. Inside are a number of fine monuments to the Touchets, Lords Audley and their successors as Lords of Markeaton the Mundys; of especial note are the dazzling monumental embellishments in Blue John, Chellaston Alabaster and a host of other marbles and polished limestones, paid for by the Mundys and in the main executed by R.G.Lomas of King Street, Derby. L9429

in 1404 – began to rebuild their timber-framed seat at the other end of the village. In the event only the notable gatehouse was started. The Mackworth's estate eventually passed to the Curzons of Kedleston.

Enclosure took place in 1763, when 2,490 acres was enclosed. One result of this was the creation of Humbleton Farm to the west and New Zealand Farm to the south-west. The latter became a suburb of Derby (qv.) as did Humbleton, for this 450 acre farm was acquired from the Clark-Maxwell family, who inherited it after the death of Mrs Mundy, by the Corporation in 1948. Although about four streets had been built upon another parcel of the farm, west of the Ring Road (Kingsway estate) before the war, (all these houses being for sale), the majority of the area was built on from 1948 to 1966 or so. This was almost entirely council housing: out of 2,660 houses only 213 were privately owned. The estate housed over 10,000 people and was set out on an irrational curvilinear plan which makes finding almost anything absurdly difficult, especially with the majority of streets named, unexpectedly, after places in and around London. The estate is served by one Anglican church, St Francis, which served a new parish carved out from that of All Saints' Mackworth in 1954, as well as Congregational (URC) and Roman Catholic churches. There is also an old folks' home, 30 shops (of which only nine were not built for letting by the council), three pubs, schools (one now a higher educational college) and a filling station. The trolley bus network was extended into the estate 8 June 1952 (to Prince

Not far from the church, a few hundred yards along Lower Road, stands the isolated late fifteenth-century gatehouse commonly called Mackworth Castle. Thomas Mackworth of Mackworth (d.1445) moved to Empingham Hall, Rutland, which his wife brought him. Although the family never returned to live in Derbyshire, John Mackworth who built the gatehouse seems to have contemplated such a move, but died suddenly in 1489 having erected only the shell of the gatehouse of a projected new seat. All sold to Sir Nathaniel Curzon during the Civil War, about 240 years before Richard Keene took this delightful photograph. L11346

Further reading:

Anon.,	*All Saints' Church, Mackworth, A Guide* (Derby, n.d. c.1990)
Bailey, G.	*Mackworth Castle* in Derbyshire Archaeological Journal XXXIII (1911) 205f.
Craven, M. & Stanley, M.	*The Derbyshire Country House* (Breedon, 1991) 135-36.
Farnsworth, D.	*From Mearca to Clark-Maxwell* (Derby, Breedon, 1987)
Kerry, C.	*Mackworth, Its Castle and Owners* in Derbyshire Archaeological Journal XI (1989) 1 f.
Lucas, R.	*The Manor of Markeaton, Mackworth and Allestree 1650-1851* (Derby 1995)
Zielonko, Mrs (Ed.)	*Mackworth Estate Jubilee; A Social History* (Derby 1980)

Charles Avenue) and 26 July 1953 (to Morden Green) and these were replaced by motor buses 9 September 1967. The area of the estate was included into the Derby boundary by special Act of Parliament, although the old village (certainly part of Derby in ancient times

The other element of Mackworth, quite apart from the old village (since the middle ages outside Derby) is the huge estate built on Humbleton Farm. This area, bounded by Kingsway, Ashbourne Road and the GN Railway was once the Markeaton estate home farm, purchased from her heirs shortly after the death of Mrs Emily Georgiana Mundy in 1929. By the outbreak of war Brackensdale Avenue, Greenland Avenue, Lilac Avenue and Laburnum Grove had been laid out, some boasting a series of flat-roofed art-deco style semis, built 1939. The remainder of the estate, mainly municipal housing, re-started building 1949 and by 1953 its first phase was complete. The photograph shows two small groups of private housing east of Enfield Road going up about 1954. The trees of Markeaton Park are visible in the background. L2148

A view of that point, towards the western edge of the estate, where Edgware Road (left) and Drayton Avenue (right) diverge. The photographer has his back to Henley Green. View taken 1961. Almost all the post-war streets in the Mackworth estate have London-derived names. L2149

A group of employees of A.E.Hibbs & Sons, of Lodge Lane, Derby pause during work on a children's playground on the estate, 1954. L2084

by attachment to the lost parish of St Mary) was never included even in the 1968 boundary extension and remains an agreeably rural backwater to this day.

Markeaton

Name: *Marcheton* in 1086, Old English = 'Mearca's farm'.

MARKEATON was a single manor held in 1086 by Hugh d'Avranches, Earl of Chester and sub-tenanted by his seneschal Goscelin, ancestor of the Touchet family who resided there until 1516 when the estate was sold to the Mundys. In fact, after the Conquest, Hugh may have at first held a dominant position in Derbyshire, including Derby itself, but a subsequent fall from grace seems to have left him only with Markeaton and its outliers (qv. Allestree, Mackworth) in Derbyshire and Henry

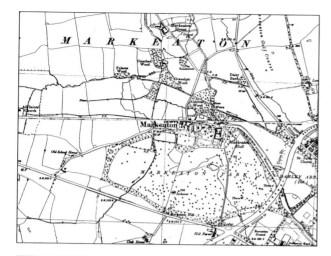

A view in Markeaton Lane *c*.1900; a Hansom cab poses for the photographer. Why and who is information now lost to us. L692

Markeaton Hall, east front, seen in 1961, three years before its highly regrettable destruction by the Borough Council. It was at least the third house on the site, and was erected in 1754-55 by James Denstone of Derby (1724-80) for Wrightson Mundy.

de Ferrers the dominant Lord in Derby and the county in his place.

At the time of Domesday Book, too, there was a village and church at Markeaton although neither really survived. The church was probably replaced by that subsequently erected at Mackworth and was itself incorporated into the hall at Markeaton as a private chapel. The village was probably much reduced in medieval times for reasons we can only guess at (cf. Cottons) and what remained was later moved from its original position by the creation of the park in the 1770s by William Emes of Bowbridge Fields. Of those houses which do remain in the village (immediately outside the hall's west gate) two at least are early eighteenth century in date, so the 'migration' of the village may have been gradual.

The estates acquired by the Mundys in 1516 stretched almost into central Derby – to Nuns' Street on the north of Friar Gate and Uttoxeter Old Road – including several suburbs treated separately here: New Zealand, Mackworth, California and the West End.

The Hall (rebuilt in 1516 and replaced in 1754-55) and park remained until 1929 when Mrs Mundy died, leaving the 2,765 acre estate to her kinsman W.G.Clark-Maxwell and the Hall with 16 acres of gardens to the council with a stipulation that they should be put to some use for the benefit of Derby's citizens. The Hall was, however, demolished in 1964. The council also purchased 211 acres of the park and some other land from the Clark-Maxwells at the same time, and the parkland is now a potentially delightful

About 1790 an extra wing was added to the Hall – seen here on the right – perhaps to the designs of George Moneypenny the younger. The new entrance was originally graced by a columned portico, but in *c.1890* Francis Mundy commissioned a conservatory porch from Messenger & Co of Loughborough. The redundant protico was re-erected at the end of the west walk as an eyecatcher, where it remains. L2489

public park, marred only by a plethora of surviving World War Two army buildings. The lake has been widened, the A38 poked through the park's southern spur and various other indignities have been visited upon it, but still the fossilised ridge and furrow of Markeaton's defunct medieval village can be discerned as well as much of Emes' striking landscape of a later, more specious age.

As with Mackworth estate, 100% land ownership by the council after 1930 effectively rendered it part of the Borough. Later legislation regularised this position. The enclosure, as at Mackworth, was achieved as early as 1763.

Further reading:
Craven, M. & Stanley, M.   *The Derbyshire Country House* (Derby, Breedon 1988) 136-39
Farnsworth, D.   *From Mearca to Clark-Maxwell* (Derby, Breedon, 1987)
Lucas, R.   *The Manor of Markeaton, Mackworth and Allestree 1650-1851* (Derby 1995)

Below: In Mrs Mundy's time local residents were free to stroll in the 117 acre park. This scene of the footbridge, from a turn-of-the-century postcard, depicts a typically favourite beauty spot, today barely recognisable thanks to the 'municipalisation' of the park after the Borough Council acquired it *c.*1929-30. L1024

In the 1970s the government of Harold Wilson decided to improve the A38(T) Exeter-Leeds trunk road. This involved slicing through Littleover, Mickleover, California and Allestree and 'improving the stretch of Ring Road through the Park at Markeaton'. No amount of vociferous protest deterred the planners. This photograph of 1975 shows the then Secretary of State for the Environment Rt. Hon. Anthony Crossland PC, MP, with the then MP for Derby North, Philip Whitehead viewing, with bored indifference, the effect of changes in Markeaton Park with the help of some self-confident local bureaucrats.

The Markeaton and Mackworth Brooks join by Aldercar Wood, north of the hall, and Emes dammed the watercourse near this point to create a pair of Serpentine lakes, to ornament his parkland. In the 1930s these lakes were 'improved' to make them suitable for boating and safe for fishing. This 1950s postcard showing the view south from the big lake highlights such activities, and is also strong on swans.

At the end of the park nearest to Derby, the landscape and the Mundys had combined to keep the insalubrious West End at bay. The lower lake penetrated beyond the east lodge (once a pretty building by Joseph Pickford) to Markeaton Street and Nuns' Mill. Unfortunately the coming of the Ring Road in the early 1930s sundered these easterly parts of the park from the rest. This view of February 1932 shows Queensway under construction in the park. L2145

Mickleover

Name: In 1011 and 1086: *Ufre:* a year later (1087 *Ufram Majorem,* later (1386) *Michelovre.* Old English for '(Great) Ridge' cf. Littleover.

I N 1011 King Aethelred ('The Unready') granted Morcar 'thegn of the Seven Boroughs' five substantial properties in Mickleover. Before 1066 it had returned to the Crown, and by 1086 William the Conqueror had granted it to Burton Abbey. It was at that time a large and rich manor with attached outliers of Littleover, Findern and Potlock – the latter now a deserted medieval village. It also had

Mickleover church was founded in the twelfth century by the Abbot of Burton and the existing building is largely of earlier fourteenth-century date. However, the improving restorer H.I.Stevens moved seamlessly on from St Peter's Littleover to All Saints' Mickleover in 1858-59, rebuilding much and adding more. The result is depicted here in a Richard Keene view taken in the 1880s. Hard by the tower stands Mickleover Manor, built 1849-62.

In 1820 the Revd Frederick Emanuel Hippolyte Curzon was appointed vicar by Sir Robert Wilmot of Chaddesden, Bt., the joint patron. This extraordinary man was eldest of five children born out of wedlock to Nathaniel, 2nd Lord Scarsdale and Felicite Anne de Wattines; four others were born after their marriage in 1798, from one of whom the present Lord Scarsdale, indeed, descends. Frederick, a notorious spendthrift, was rector for over 51 years, and one of his first extravagances was a handsome new Regency Vicarage (1821) perhaps built to designs by Richard Leaper. It is seen here in decay about 1972. Facing the Square, it would have made a handsome private residence or felicitous flats, but was demolished soon afterwards and replaced by a block of flats of extreme banality. L5800

Along the east side of the vicarage runs northward a street once called Cattle Hill (OS maps) a mutation of the much more ancient Cackle Hill (from Old English *caecca* = 'hump' + hill), but renamed by municipal improvers later as the more prosaic Vicarage Road. It ran to Holly End, then turned east ending up in Station Road. In this view taken in the 1890s Cackle Hill Farm, then tenanted by William Baldwin, is seen as an agreeable seventeenth-century gabled brick edifice. L3335

control of lands in eight other nearby Derbyshire villages and in Derby itself. The position in 1086 was much inferior to 20 years before as the taxable value had fallen 60% and included the *sites* of two mills – clear evidence of destruction. One mill however, at Rough Heanor (Old English, 'rough ridge') in the parish, was quickly repaired and let to a kinsman of the Abbey's tenant Humphrey de Touques. Although a church is not mentioned in Domesday Book, the earlier Charter granting the manor to the Abbey of Burton mentions churches and chapels in Mickleover, Littleover, Findern and Potlock, so either they had fallen into disuse or (more likely) had merely been omitted from Domesday Book (as had two at least of Derby's churches) for some long-lost administrative reason. The present church of All Saints' has fabric dating from the earlier fourteenth century, and it may be it was completely rebuilt at that time, as it was again in 1858.

Another view of Cackle (or Cattle) Hill, this time looking in the opposite direction towards the rise which separates this area – Holly End – from The Square. From a postcard of c.1904. The photographer is standing where the road swings at a right angle towards Station Road. Every child in the street has come out to pose for the camera!

West Drive, once pitched, was quickly built up, and by 1938 was also lined with south-facing 'builders manual' London semis, as in this postcard, one of a series chronicling the suburban growth of Mickleover in that era, just prior to World War Two.

The main estate in the village came into the hands of the Newtons (a branch of those of Chaddesden) by early in the seventeenth century, and they remained the chief landowners, building the present Manor 1849-62, until they sold up after World War One and retired to Lockington. By the early nineteenth century, however, a number of other people were acquiring land and building elegant villas, which still survive.

The coming of the railway in 1876-78 began the suburban expansion of Mickleover,

Almost at the same scene, c.1936. The fields on the right in the previous view were sold by the Newtons (later the Curzons) of Mickleover Manor – who had sensibly moved away to Lockington – for development. These bland semis were the result. Vicarage Road, as it was soon to become was extended northwards and West Drive pitched to connect it again to Station Road. The old connection, off camera to the left, was renamed Park Road.

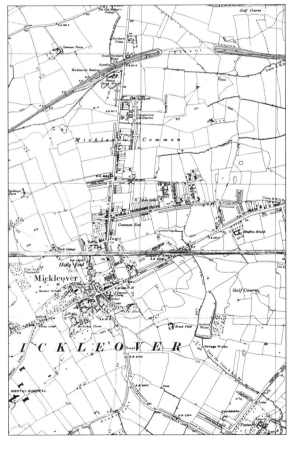

Back in front of the Vicarage, of course, was the pleasant Market Place of Mickleover (later called The Square), with its Georgian cottages, seen here in a 1920s summer evening view from the church gate.

a process which continued until the first years of the present century and resumed once the Newton estate began to be broken up some 20 years later. The common land, lying between Mickleover and Littleover, was enclosed in 1790.

Despite the rapid expansion of Mickleover by 1939 and further building in the later 1950s, and 1960s, Derby did not absorb the village until 1968, which meant that the Uttoxeter Road trolley bus service, inaugurated on 13 August 1933 only ran as far as then newly-built Corden Avenue, in Rough Heanor, just within the Borough boundary as expanded in 1928. The service was replaced by motorbuses from 26 November 1966 and with the boundary extension two years later, the anomaly of Corporation buses stopping short of the village was ended. The other side of the coin was the withdrawal of regular passenger trains from the station from 4 December 1939 and all trains from 2 August 1959. The station also closed to goods traffic 3 February 1964, although goods trains passed through to Burton upon Trent until 6 May 1968.

Since 1968 further development has expanded Mickleover, especially north of Devonshire Drive on Silverhill Farm, and on the land west of Uttoxeter Road below Cawdy Hill and bounded by the new A38 and A516 link roads, driven through the parish (and drastically affecting the Mickleover Golf Course) in 1972-73.

The coming of the Toyota works nearby in the early 1990s has also led to the construction of a four star hotel (the Mickleover Court) at the north end of the village, which finally opened in 1994. It actually stands a few feet outside the City boundary, for the land of the parish west of the village was omitted from the 1968 boundary changes.

From the other side, the Square is here seen on 14 October 1932. The only change in the decade since the previous view was taken is the decorative treatment above the shop front of the building on the extreme left and the appearance of a cast-iron electrical switchbox on the site of the drinking fountain to control the new-fangled electric lighting installed a few months before. The grass in the Market Place has been replaced by asphalt – no doubt to facilitate car parking. Note the Masons' Arms opposite the church. Cattle Hill begins by the vicarage wall, extreme right. L3340

This also left the County Lunatic Asylum (built to designs of Henry Duesbury 1849) – latterly Pastures Hospital – outside the city. This institution, architecturally emasculated post-war by the NHS, closed and at the time of writing the future of the large and prominent site is highly uncertain.

Further reading:

Brix, V.H.	*The Story of Mickleover and its Church* (Derby 1951)
Craven, M. & Stanley, M.	*The Derbyshire Country House* (Breedon, Derby 1991) 143-45
Ford H.G. & Ravensdale A.G.	*The Mickleover Story* (Derby 1969)
Watson, S.	*Mickleover and Littleover, A History* (Ashbourne 1993)

From the Market Place runs also The Hollow – not as pretty as The Hollow in neighbouring Littleover once was, but still an attractive backwater. It is flanked by Regency Ivy House on one side and a very fine (and recently restored) sixteenth-century timber-framed yeoman's house, below which are a range of early nineteenth-century labourers' cottages seen here in this turn-of-the century postcard view. L12512

Slightly nearer Derby is another street parallel to the Hollow – Limes Avenue. As its name suggests it is a road leading to The Limes, a white stuccoed Regency villa of some elegance. Like the upper part of The Hollow the street was once lined with old, vernacular brick cottages. L3336

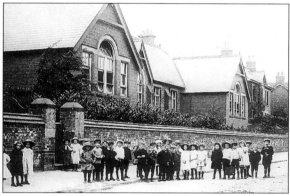

The Limes Lodge, Limes Avenue, 1970. The detailing and proportions of the pretty Gothic lodge suggest the same hand for it (and The Limes) as designed the very similar double lodge at The Pastures, Littleover. Assuming that in both cases lodge and house are by the same hand, The Limes and its lodge can confidently be attributed by the amateur architect, serial mayor, banker and tanner Alderman Richard Leaper (1759-1838). It was built c.1828-29. A very similar house, possibly also by Leaper, is Mickleover House off Orchard Street, built 1824 for Alderman Samuel Rowland. L5575

A few yards from the junction of Limes Avenue and Uttoxeter Road stands the former Public Elementary School, seen here with most of its infant customers posing in front of it about 1910. It was first built under the terms of the School Board Act in 1880 but was considerably rebuilt and enlarged in 1907 by J.W.Horton. Mrs Beare, the infants' mistress, seems to have modestly excluded herself from the photograph. The building still stands. L3853

Separated from the school by two modest late Victorian villas was the post office. If the infants from the school were safely corralled in the road for the previous photograph, it would appear that the junior boys had descended on the post office to buy chocolate! The shop, (c.1910) then run by Mr Freckleton, seems to have been built out from a third 1880s brick villa. Even today it still flourishes as a shop. L11675

A little further along again and one encounters the Vine Inn, then a lowly beer house not long taken over by Messrs. Stretton of Derby. It had for many years a 'living sign' as here – a vine branch growing on its façade. Apart from its loss, it has not much changed from this angle since, although a considerable extension had recently been added to the west side. The building on the far left has recently been replaced too. Yet again, the place is alive with children! From a postcard of c.1910. L11674

The Vine stands close to the corner of Station Road, the other side of which stands yet another Regency House, Mickleover Lodge, pictured here *c.*1906. This was built in the 1820s (but by a much less fashionable architect than The Limes) for George Wade (born 1796) a gentleman farmer who was the only freeholder in the village of any consequence apart from the Newtons of The Manor during most of the nineteenth century. George's brother Samuel (1806-1878) built Ivy House. They also farmed The Meadows. By the time George Wade died, his eldest son George Hayward Wade had moved to The Warren, Loughborough, and the house was let to John Hodson and afterwards to Sydney Leech, elder son of Alderman Charles Leech who had been Mayor of Derby 1885-86; he was a director of Leech, Neal & Co paint manufacturers (qv.). Much later it became Our Lady of Lourdes Catholic church, and still stands in the grounds of its replacement. L1037, 1162

Station Road led off from Uttoxeter Road northwards towards the station, having been created out of an existing lane and some farm tracks when the Great Northern Railway was built in 1876-77. This view was taken in 1930 from the top of the first rise (near where the ambulance station is today) looking towards Franco's shop on the corner of Park Road. On the left, private houses built in the early 1920s; on the right, council houses then virtually new.

Further down Station Road, and the housing stock is earlier. In this postcard view, looking north, of *c.*1910 the road is as yet only partly made up. At Oaklands, in Station Road, had lived Arthur Coke-Hill (1847-1907) architect of the Mechanics' Institute, Derby and of many of the larger late Victorian villas in Mickleover. His son, Lionel (1872-1941) – an engineer at Bass' – lived nearby at 90 Western Road. L4034

Beyond the built-up part of Station Road, but still south of the railway was the Mill on Mickleover Common, a bleak tract of land dividing Mickleover from Mackworth. In the earlier nineteenth century it was in the hands of George Hill, an uncle of the architect, but was later run jointly with Sunnyside, a farm. This 1950s view shows it long out of use and truncated. The new development of Mill Lane and Mill Croft (early 1970s) now covers the site with Onslow Road in front of it. L3342

Another view, taken *c.*1938 in virtually the same place as the preceding (left). The houses have hardly changed, but the road is wider and fully metalled. Note the single decker bus. L1034

An aerial view of the railway, Station Road and the station (left, middle distance) taken 2 June 1963. Centrepiece of the view is the newly-completed Nestlé factory, built here to enable the workforce to use the trains to travel to work – a forlorn hope as it turned out! Opposite it, the Great Northern Inn built 1889, the first landlord of which was Henry Jarrett. The factory has since passed to Rolls-Royce. In the background (top) Common Farm. L4924

Left: Development of the land north of Western Road and east of Station Road began in 1936, but only part of Devonshire Drive, North Avenue and Moorland Road were completed before war broke out. The remainder of the development did not start until the 1950s and continued for almost 20 years. This view shows all that was completed of Devonshire Drive in 1937. It was so named because at the enclosure of 1790, the Duke of Devonshire was allocated 46 acres in this area.

Station Road's existence was entirely thanks to the provision of Mickleover for Radbourn Station by the Great Northern Railway on their Ilkeston-Egginton Junction line opened on All Fools' Day 1878, and seen here *c.*1904. The first stationmaster was F.Seymour. The last goods train called 3 February 1964 and the line closed 6 May 1968. However the station yard, suitably modified, remained in use for experimental train testing from closure until 1990. The station buildings, however, were converted into an agreeable residence for Mr Barry Sims, director of music at the nearby former Bishop Lonsdale College (now part of the University) in the 1970s. Passenger services never resumed after the war. L9141

Running east from Station Road, behind Mickleover Lodge and parallel with Uttoxeter Road is Western Road, created from land sold by the Wades *c.*1898-1900. This view is eastwards from near to the Station Road end taken October 1930. L3338

Slightly to the north of Moorland Road, East Avenue and the immediately contiguous part of Chestnut Avenue were completed in the later 1930s, as this 1938 view of East Avenue testifies.

New Normanton

Name: *See* Normanton

OR the early history of Normanton (qv.) see under that heading. New Normanton is that part of St Peter's Parish, Derby (in which Normanton-by-Derby for so many centuries lay) west of the Litchurch boundary (qv.) and south of Burton Road. Its southern boundary ultimately became approximately co-terminous with the Ring Road.

Little development had taken place before about 1865, but thereafter sales of land by various Normanton freeholders enabled development to proceed quite quickly. Most of the area had been common until 1769 when it had been enclosed. Of the subsequent owners, none had been more assiduous in acquiring land from other awardees than the Goodales, who later had a lead mill on Normanton Road. The sale of James Wyatt's Ordnance depot nearby in the early 1820s also gave London silk throwster Ambrose Moore a freehold. Between 1848 and 1884 land sales enabled the new suburb to expand: the estate of John Goodale sold in 1848; Revd Charles Wright of Offerton, Cheshire (vicar and patron of St Peter's) died 1865 and 1,024 acres were sold 1 November 1865 of which Cottons Farm (380 acres) and New House Farm (248 acres) sold to their tenants. Peartree Farm, owned by the Peach family, was sold through the bankruptcy of the Peaches in 1865 – hence a well-known sub-district, partly in New Normanton, partly in Litchurch (qv.). A year later Mrs Goodale sold more land, followed by the heirs of Ambrose Moore (partly acquired by Offiler's brewery), Richard Sale (*c.*1867), John Willn (*c.*1873), Joseph Millington, market gardener (1874), Sir John Porte's Charity (34 acres acquired from the enclosure, 1875), Col. Newdigate of West Hallam and Arbury (April

From Derby one enters New Normanton where Normanton Road, Green Lane, Babington Lane and Burton Road met – at Little City. Travel along Normanton Road and you are in a suburb considered very genteel when it was laid out gradually over the fields which divided Derby from the old village of Normanton from the 1860s. This view was taken *c.*1968 from the mouth of Loudon Street looking across to the former Tower Supermarket on Ambrose Street corner. This was later Kwik Save and has spread over Ambrose Street completely. It replaced Offiler's brewery (taken over by Bass 1965 and rapidly demolished) which had been expanded into Ambrose Moore's bankrupt Depot silk mill in the late nineteenth century.

Cross Normanton Road and enter Ambrose Street (not really possible today) and this view has largely vanished, the houses nearest the camera having been cleared for a car-park. Ahead is Bainbrigge Street, with Upper Bainbrigge Street curving away to the left, by the rather superior house on the corner – no.37, built by a man called Mason, a grocer, around 1865 and still standing. Ambrose Moore was a Twyford-born silk throwster who bought the redundant Ordnance Depot on Normanton Road (originally built in 1806 by James Wyatt) and converted it into a silk mill. Ambrose, Moore, Dashwood and Bainbrigge Streets were built by him to house his workforce. L11667

1879) and Benjamin Edge of New House Farm (1884).

In 1878, 203 acres of Normanton – mainly comprising the fast-expanding new suburb – were transferred to Derby; the area had supported 50 people in 1850, but 27 years later 2,750 on some thirty streets, 23 of which had been laid out 1875-77. New parishes were carved out of St Peter's to serve these people, too: St Chad 1878 and St Thomas 1883. The Catholic church of St Joseph followed in 1897 and numerous dissenting congregations founded chapels.

Yet the area was almost exclusively artisan and *petit bourgeois* in those days, Normanton Road itself being considered 'very respectable'; the grandfather of the late Viscount Wakefield resided there for many years. The area was served by horse trams to and from the Normanton Hotel from 28 May 1881, and the service was electrified 26 July 1904, to which were added further services to the Cavendish (8 September) and from Cavendish to Osmaston Road (5 September 1905). These were replaced by trolley buses 17 March 1934, and other routes then began, eg Cavendish to Browning Circle 3 June 1935, Sinfin Lane from Normanton Barracks 30 August 1943, all replaced between 1960 and 1966 by motor buses. In 1890 the Midland Railway opened a station in Osmaston (qv.) called, however, Peartree and Normanton, to help its own employees get to work easily. It closed in 1968 but re-opened eight years later when a service from Sinfin (Central) to Matlock via Derby was inaugurated. The station was 'improved' in 1993-94.

Since the 1970s gradual demolition of the property on some of the older streets has been undertaken to be replaced by low-rise Housing Association residences. In some cases (as

in Upper Dale Road) the entire street layout has been changed. In 1993 the City Challenge initiative set up Derby Pride Ltd with much grant money from Central funds to improve New Normanton and Litchurch, both areas having become very run down since World War Two. This has done wonders for the appearance of Normanton Road, if nothing else; the oldest (and thus the handsomest) houses in Rose Hill Street still appear to be in terminal decay, however.

The first major divergence from Normanton Road is Mill Hill Lane which leads to St Chad's Road, laid out c.1880 and embellished with a worthy, stolid church which gave its name to the road, having been designed by H.C.Turner and completed in 1882. Gordon Road, on the corner of which St Chad's stands (or stood, for the Church of England has barbarous plans to demolish it) contains the Roman Catholic Church of St Joseph, built of brick in 1879 to designs of James Hart, and rebuilt in 1896-97. To its left in this view by local photographer F.W.Scarratt (c.1903) is the presbytery, also in a Lombardic Gothic style. In the 1970s this church was replaced by an ultra-modern one in the grounds of Mill Hill House nearby, also dedicated to St Joseph. This church then was taken over by a Polish congregation and re-dedicated to St Maksymilian Kolbe. L9418

Gordon Road : a nearby corner shop at no.19 – long de-commissioned, still has its 1880s shop window and bears a contemporary trademark of Stretton's Brewery, Manchester Street, Derby. The photograph was taken on 28 February 1957.

Further along St Chad's Road begins to rise gently before coming out on Overdale Road. The streets run off to the south, including Cromwell Road, seen here, where house building, interrupted by World War One resumed in the 1920s and 1930s. This view is of nos.20-24, very plain 1920s semis, taken in October 1925. Note the roof of a similar house in Hamilton Road behind. L12636

Where St Chad's Road and Overdale Road meet there is a round, iron-fenced 'island' of bushes forming a further junction with Whitaker Road and Carlton Road. Whitaker Road, extreme left in this 1948 view by Hurst & Wallace, was laid out c.1862 as part of the Littleover Hill estate. It took over 50 years for all the houses to be built, however. Carlton Road (where the photographer is standing) was pitched c.1900 and extended a decade or so later. All the houses in view were built c.1900. L2107

A little on the east of Normanton Park and one encounters the area known as Cavendish after the name of the large hotel erected in 1898 on the corner of Upper Dale Road and Walbrook Road. The area in front of it sees the conjunction of not only these streets but also Derby Lane, Stenson Road and Almond Street and the entire area takes its name from the pub. This picture, taken from Stenson Road, with its neat K2 telephone box and the trolley bus wires, was taken c.1934-5. The Normanton Co-op store is clearly visible, left. L2583

A very similar view but much earlier showing two tramcars passing on Upper Dale Road. L021

Ascend Whitaker Road to its more westerly junction with Burton Road, and one finds largish villas set amid bosky pleasure grounds. Many of the latter are the work of the landscape gardeners William Barron Ltd, and the house in this view (The Cedars) was also one of these. It is situated at the south-east corner of Burton Road and is today the University School of Occupational Therapy. It was built in 1862 to designs by William Giles and was the residence of the chief constable Col. William Addis Delacombe for over 25 years before being purchased by Brig. W.W.Bemrose in the 1900s. This photograph was taken from the rear about the time the Bemroses sold it c.1950. L11215

Further reading:

Craven, M.
Illustrated History of Derby, (Derby, Breedon, 1988) 195-98, 20-23, 214, 214, 231, 236.

Payne, C.J.
Derby Churches Old and New (Derby 1893) 65-73

A much earlier view of the hotel itself with tramcars approaching up Lower Dale Road (left) and Walbrook Road (right). The carefully posed driver, left, is Mr Payne, and the date is shortly after the track was laid in front of the pub in September 1905.

The Derby Pavilion, a large timber music hall was destroyed by fire in January 1929. After that, a pitch-and-putt course was laid out until 1937 when the Cavendish Cinema was built on the site for £30,000. The first film shown (28 December 1937) was *For You Alone*. Taken over by Rank in 1942 and closed 19 December 1960 after a screening of locally-shot *Sons and Lovers*. After another interval the site was cleared and in 1965 a Fine Fare supermarket was built, which later became Gateway and in 1994 Somerfield. The photograph was taken in the early 1950s.

Normanton Park, seen here to mark the opening by the Duke of Devonshire 4 September 1909. The park was 30 acres and the pretty pavilion, designed by Borough architect John Ward, bears a John Smith & Sons turret clock. L12336

Below: This view shows the pavilion *c.*1934, when it was a café with a glimpse beyond the southern gates of the park to newly-built Warwick Avenue and the municipal houses on its far side. Today the park is all rather run down and forlorn. L2607, 3490

The last parts of New Normanton to be built over were those fields south of Walbrook Road – visible here on the left – with Cameron Road right of centre. A 33 acre parcel of land bounded by Village Street and what later became St Thomas' Road, Walbrook Road and Brunswick Street was sold at auction 12 November 1884, following the death of Normanton farmer Benjamin Edge (1800-1884). It was bought for £7,900 by Derby attorney Henry Cummings who developed the area over the following 20 years. This photograph is by Richard Keene junior in 1899; Cooks Directory for 1898, under all the streets visible has 'Houses Building'. Some of Mr Edge's farm building near Derby Lane (left) still stand at this date.

New Zealand

Name: Taken from the Commonwealth Country as a farm name by the Chandos-Poles, probably to commemorate the Treaty of Waitangi (1840).

THE land between Ashbourne Road and the later course of the Great Northern Railway (alongside the Bramble Brook) was mainly split between the Chandos-Pole estate and some holdings of the Bemrose family. In 1851 much of it was purchased by the Freehold Land Society, a building club, which by 1852 had laid out Bass, Peel, Cobden and Langley Streets, and parts of Heyworth, Radbourne, Morley, Bright and Surrey Streets. Stepping and Slack Lanes were, however, pre-existing

The northern boundary of the suburb is formed by the Ashbourne Road, seen here early in 1924 looking west. In the distance there is no roundabout, for the scene comfortably pre-dates the Ring Road. Just the little early eighteenth-century squatters' cottage (right) which miraculously survived into the 1950s and some mid-nineteenth century cottages by the Travellers Rest inn, itself renovated at about this time and still today serving its best bitter straight from the jug! L2256

farm access tracks later improved. By 1860 building had commenced, including three inns: the New Zealand Arms (corner of Peel and Langley Streets) later the Cobden Arms (corner of Morley Street and Cobden Street) and not forgetting the Crescent (corner of Wild Street and Campion Street) the latter named after the dominant motif on the Chandos-Pole coat of arms.

Most of the streets were named after local MPs – Bass, Heyworth, Plimsoll etc – and Whig statesmen. Radbourne and Langley Streets were named after two Chandos-Pole properties (the street named after the family was on the *North* side of Ashbourne Road!);

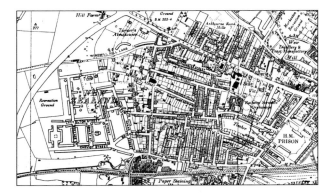

Howe, Lloyd and Arnold Streets are Bemrose ancestors, and the remainder are various minor local worthies mainly connected with the Howes.

On the site (we are told) of one of the windmills which gives its name to Windmill Hill Lane was built 1884-85 the church of St Barnabas, to serve the new New Zealand Parish to be carved out of that of St John, Bridge Street. It was completed over a number of subsequent years, all to designs by Arthur Coke-Hill of Mickleover (1847-1907). The font, from West Hallam Hall, was reputed to have been used by the martyr Edmund Campion – hence the Street name. At this time too, was built the Railway Servants' Orphanage (St Christopher's) and in 1865 Messrs Stretton of Manchester took over Eyre's brewery Ashbourne Road, expanding in the 1880s into a new brewery and maltings designed by G.H. Sheffield, laying out Manchester Street to accommodate it.

The housing of New Zealand varies from artisans' cottages of a basic type to the east of St Barnabas', and middle-class villas beyond. The whole development was in place by about 1890, prevented from expansion west by the Borough boundary which then ran down the later courses of Morley and Hawke Streets. This shifted in 1928-29, allowing development of

On the south side of Ashbourne Road the Midland Railway built its orphanage in 1877, to designs by their own architects Charles Trubshaw and A.A.Langley. The latter, actually a civil engineer, was brother-in-law of Sir Clement Bowring, Derby Tory grandee, and – more to the point – son-in-law of Sir James Allport, general manager of the Railway company. It superseded a converted Regency villa on London Road, rented from the widow of Mr Etches the cheese factor. This fine French château-style building was, in 1982, demolished and replaced by a much simpler group of small buildings, but the home closed completely a decade later, after which the University erected one of its numerous economy-class student residences on the site which would be a perfectly good building were it not in an important conservation area. L9628

Municipal housing to continue to Kingsway and beyond into Humbleton Farm (qv. Mackworth) after World War Two.

Further reading:
Craven, M.
Inns and Taverns of Derby (Derby, Breedon, 1992) 14-15, 52, 55, 108, 164 & 169.
Payne, C.J.
Derby Churches Old and New (Derby 1893) 59-64

Once upon a time, Windmill Hill Lane left the Ashbourne Road by the toll bar (its canted-fronted toll booth survives) and was a farm track which meandered over the edge of Humbleton Farm to the mill by Windmill Hill wood. Its course is now cut by Kingsway, obliterated by Highgate Green, Mackworth estate (where once it turned west) and the wood now lies under the area between Isleworth Drive and Sevenoaks Avenue. The part of the lane in New Zealand was built up on the north side with municipal houses which were built immediately beyond Rose Place (a court of cottages almost behind the Travellers' Rest), past Bass Street. The first photograph is looking down Windmill Hill Lane in February 1957; the second looking the other way from a spot not far removed from the first, was taken in July 1953, early in the morning, and shows the rural ambience surviving, even then. (Courtesy Don Farnsworth Esq. L3240-1.)

Normanton-by-Derby

Name: *Normanestune* (1086), Old English: 'The farm of the Northmen'(i.e. Vikings).

CLEARLY its name suggests that Normanton must have been founded by Norse settlers after the fall of Mercia in 874 and probably before they were ejected by Queen Aethelflaeda in 917. It may be however that they took over an existing Saxon settlement of greater Northworthy and merely renamed it.

Like Chellaston, Osmaston and Cottons, a little land (a Carucate)at Normanton was attached to the Royal Manor of Melbourne. The settlement consisted in 1066 of three

At the top of Sinfin Lane was Normanton Barracks, built to house the 95th (Derbyshire) Regt, in 1874-77. They closed in 1963 and were demolished in 1982, later to be replaced by Michael Sassoon's outrageously inventive Oast House Hotel (1989), a bowling alley, cinema and fried chicken emporium: *Sic Transit gloria mundi!* This view of *c.*1905 is from a postcard of the armoury, a grim brick tower. L12492/19

Below: The other view is of the main parade ground – The Square – taken at the same time. The two buildings behind the soldiers were Chatsworth and Marabout barrack blocks. L12492/27

manorial estates held by Leofric and Theodoric (probably Saxons) and by Gamel (probably of Norse descent). In 1086 Amalric de Chellaston held all three manors from Henry de Ferrers, along with a little land belonging to Normanton which lay in Stenson (Twyford parish). The subsequent history of the ownership of these three estates is highly complex, but they eventually came to the families of Sacheverell of Stanton by Bridge, Folcher (followed by Bagshawe) and Babington. The latter managed to acquire the greater part, selling to the Beaumonts from whom the Dixies of Bosworth acquired it (and allowed the Manor House to go to ruin) passing it on to the Pochins of Barkby who sold up in the early nine-teenth century, mainly to the Goodales.

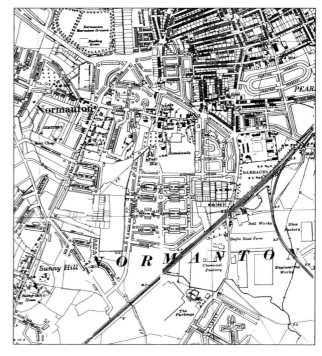

They rebuilt the elegant Pochin residence, Normanton House, now semi-derelict in the grounds of Homelands School, early in the nineteenth century.

The church must have been built very shortly after the period of the Domesday Book, for there were remains of that date in the fabric of the old chapel of St Peter, pulled down in 1861 and replaced to designs of Giles & Brookhouse of Derby, being dedicated to St Giles 13 May 1862. Normanton's ancient ties with Derby were severed when it became a separate parish in 1877. The Goodale family estates were sold in 1848 to the brothers Wright, of a family from Offerton Hall, Cheshire, one of whom, Charles, was vicar of St Peters. He thus also became his own patron, but when he died in 1865 the old manorial estate was sold, creating a number of substantial freeholds – some with largish houses, some of which acquired them – and in turn many of these were sold allowing numerous small occupiers to become owners too. At this juncture New Normanton began to grow apace (qv.) and became increasingly separate until 1879 when Derby absorbed it.

In 1874-78 new barracks were built, ultimately becoming the home of the 95th (Derbyshire) Regt., later the 2nd Battalion Sherwood Foresters (45th/95th). Normanton elected its first parish council under the new Act in 1894, but the number of councillors was reduced from seven to five in 1901 when Derby County Borough obtained a boundary extension which deprived Normanton of 190 out of a total of 1,181 acres. Of the part taken over, there were 17 newly-built streets: most of the parish council's rateable property! Almost the whole of the village was taken over in 1928, however, an event which triggered development of municipal housing on the estate of Mr Giles Austin of Homelands, a Derby grocer who died in 1929. A Grammar School was founded on the site adjacent to

The centre of the historic village is Village Street, seen here in Edwardian times looking north-west. On the left the stables of long-vanished Lake House, at the time of the photograph the residence of Captain William Friend. It was first mentioned as far back as 1724 when it was the property of Michael Willson. His descendants sold it to the Goodales of Normanton House. Opposite is the former Sunday School designed by Giles & Brookhouse and built in 1879-80. The corner nearest the camera is now a shop; the far gable now graces the Church of God of Prophecy which purchased that part of the building from the parish church in 1976. L9105

Homelands in 1937, designed by C.H.Aslin of Derby. More council houses were built on the south-facing grounds of Normanton House and more still on the site of Lake House nearby, whose owner also most opportunely died in 1929. Other houses rose up upon the site of a brickyard on the south-west corner of newly-built Warwick Avenue (the Ring Road) and Stenson Road; further new housing has replaced large nineteenth-century villas and their usually spacious grounds since the war, too, most recently on the site of The Knoll, Stenson Road.

Even today Normanton-by-Derby still retains a distinct identity, helped by the roaring madness of Kenilworth Avenue (the Ring Road) driven through just on the north side of Village Street between the wars and now grossly overloaded. It seems an effective barrier between the much-transformed village and Derby.

Nearby stands the parish church, a medieval foundation as a chapel-at-ease of St Peter's, Derby, and replaced by a new building of 1861 by Giles & Brookhouse of Derby, the broached spire echoing a somewhat dumpier version of that which had graced the previous church. In this view of 1899, looking west along Village Street, the churchyard wall is visible, left, along with a line of vernacular cottages, now largely demolished. L11055

Between the wars development in Normanton tended to be near Littleover and south of the village including Stenson Road, where this view was taken – really Sunnyhill, a mini-suburb between Normanton and Littleover named after a long-vanished farm. At left, Breedon Avenue. The tranquil scene was recorded in summer 1948.

Further reading:
Craven, M. & Stanley, M. *The Derbyshire Country House* Vol.2 (Matlock, 1984) 55
Harrison, J. *Some Account of the History of Normanton-by-Derby and its Church* (Normanton, n.d. (c.1958).
Normanton-by-Derby Local History Group *The Story of Normanton* (Derby, Breedon, 1993)
Raven, J. *Normanton-by-Derby, A Glimpse of the Past* (Derby 1988)

Ockbrook

Name: 'The brook of Occa' (Old English)

I N 1066 one Toki held the manor of Ockbrook but 20 years later it was part of the extensive holdings of Geoffrey Alselin, as was Elvaston, a chapelry of which Ockbrook church once was. However, sometime before 1620, it was esteemed a separate parish. The church is dedicated to All Saints, and a Norman font is a solitary attestation of its antiquity, although the tower too is later twelfth century and the broached spire was added a century later. The main body of the church appears to have undergone rebuilding in 1803, 1815 and 1835. The patrons were the Stanhopes of Elvaston, followed by the Lakes and Pares's of Hopwell Hall, the latter, like Borrowash and Shacklecross nearby, places closely associated with the parish. Like

A view up Victoria Avenue – the road which connects Ockbrook with Borrowash – towards Bakehouse Lane (left) where it becomes Flood Street. The prominent building on the corner is the Queen's Head inn. When this photograph was taken c.1908 the landlord was Frederick White. Another landlord of this era was the Derby artist Frank Gresley. The Queen's Head still exists – albeit drastically altered – but the scene has changed in other respects. L9131

Ockbrook itself, however, none were ever attached to Derby.

The manor was divided between two of three presumed sons of Sir Ralph Halselin *c.*1130 and half descended to the Bardolfs of Wormegay (a descendant of which family sold the portion to the Foljambes in *c.*1420) and the other to Serlo de Grendon who, with his kin, granted his share to the Abbey of Dale. At the Reformation, these shares were largely broken up amongst the freeholders, notably the Battelles, Harpurs, Keyes (of Hopwell) and Wilmots of Chaddesden.

In 1750 the Moravians started a settlement in the village, which still flourishes, complimented by its delightful Georgian buildings. One of the many inns, the Royal Oak, was in the hands of the Peet family for some three hundred years until its sale in 1912, a remarkable record. From the earlier nineteenth century, middle-class families from Derby and Long Eaton took advantage of the fragmented landowning pattern to acquire land and built elegant villas.

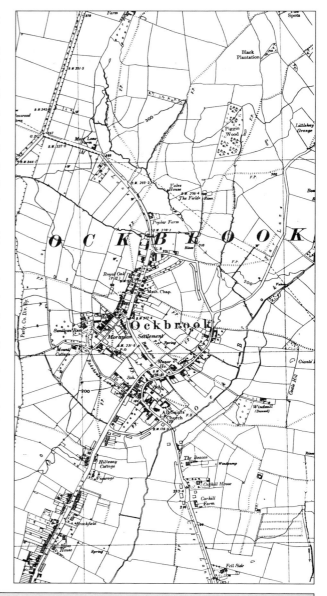

Further reading:

Johnson, M.   *Memories of Ockbrook and Borrowash* (Ilkeston 1990)

Johnson, M.   *More Memories of Ockbrook and Borrowash* (Borrowash 1991)

Johnson, M.   *Ockbrook and its Parson, Samuel Hey 1810-1852* (Borrowash 1991)

Johnson, M.   *Ockbrook in the 1820s* (Borrowash 1991)

Smith, J.L.   *Ockbrook in Old Picture Postcards* (Zaltbommel, 1985)

Osmaston-by-Derby

Name: Originally (1086) *Osmundestune* – 'Osmund's Farm' – Old English.

THE first mention of Osmaston is, as so often, in the Domesday Book, of 1086. Here the story is much as it was for Chellaston, Normanton and Cottons: one part was attached to the King's Manor of Melbourne, the rest was part of the extensive holdings of Henry de Ferrers, and after the disgrace and forfeiture of his descendant, the last Ferrers Earl of Derby, it came under the Duchy of Lancaster, as did the other places under the Ferrers sway in 1086.

The interesting thing about Osmaston is that in 1066 it was held by one Osmund – no doubt coincidence, despite that the village name derives from this very (Saxon) name. It must be borne in mind that the naming of the village probably goes back somewhat further, to an eponymous Osmund. However, Saxon families did tend to stick to the same name every other generation or so, also tending to alliterate all the names in the family, so the possibility that both Osmunds were related does exist. In Osmaston he held one manor with an outlier in Cottons, where he was also Lord. He must have been a man of some consequence, for he had also held a manor in Denby. Domesday Book names no tenant for Osmaston, yet Osmund was still around, as Kings' thegn holding a manor in Sandiacre and one in 'Chelton' (a place not fully identified, but conceivably a separate

Osmaston was one of many of Derby's village suburbs, but having been absorbed early on, the village ultimately vanished. As with most places, the settlement focussed upon church and manor house. This view of the church of St James was taken *c.*1903 and represents the results of a 'judicious restoration', as Dr Cox delicately put the thorough rebuilding it underwent in 1878. For a 'before' view see *Keene's Derby* (Breedon, Derby 1993) p.107. It had twelfth-century fabric much rebuilt in the fourteenth century, but it was pulled down to make way for the Ascot Drive trading estate. L9421

manor of Chellaston). The family continued to hold their estate in Sandiacre a century later, and it is reasonable to

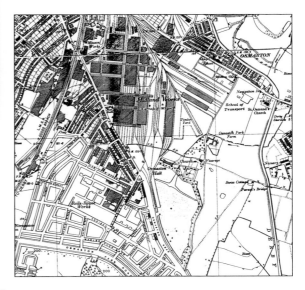

The west front of Osmaston Hall photographed by Richard Keene in 1857, when Revd Samuel Fox, Rector of Morley (d.1870) lived there. The Fox's were an Old Derby family who rented the house (but not the 3,708 acre estate) after the Wilmots became the Wilmot-Hortons and moved to Catton Hall. The house was built in 1696-98 and was demolished in 1938 by Derby Corporation. L90

assume that Osmund (in the absence of any other name) may have continued as tenant in Osmaston, and thus be progenitor of the Osmaston family. Certainly it is clear that the Osmaston Codinton and Folcher families (the latter Lords of Normanton) were all of the same stock.

Somehow, by c.1160, the manor of Osmaston had passed to Robert de Dun of Breadsall, who gave the tiny church (of St James) – a chapel of St Peter's Derby, in which parish Osmaston remained – to the Abbey of Darley. A church was probably first built shortly after 1086, for the now-vanished font (seen in 1820) was of distinctly Norman character. The remainder was early fourteenth century, but was extensively restored in 1878.

By the seventeenth century the estate was in the hands of the Wilmots – a branch of the Wilmots of Chaddesden (qv.) – and they built a small stone manor house, incorporated into a very much grander affair (which I have elsewhere attributed to Sir William Wilson, repeated as fact by someone writing in the *Derby Express* of 19 April 1995!) in 1696. In the 1840s the Wilmots – by this time baronets like their Chaddesden kinsmen – inherited Catton Hall from the Hortons, and migrated thence, letting the

On the Osmaston Road was one of the Hall's lodges, a very pretty *cottage orne,* Gothic and thatched. It had distinct affinities with that at The Limes, Mickleover, and may be by Richard Leaper as well. It was destroyed after World War Two by the creation of Ascot Drive, which follows the course of both the north and south hall drives. L12145

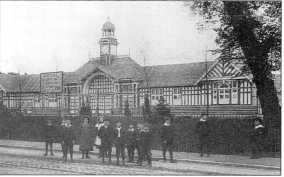

The Wilmot family were the first to allow the Royal Agricultural Society hold the Royal Show on Osmaston Park, in 1843. Another followed on 5 July 1881. The third, which was attended by Edward VII in person, was on 28 June 1906, by which time the parkland had been split between the Borough Council's ownership and that of the Midland Railway. The photograph shows the impressive prefabricated pavilion, designed in 1891 by a Mr Dennison. The entire edifice could be dismantled in two days and stored flat. This view, in Osmaston Road, was taken 26 June 1906. L4431

On 29 June 1921 the Royal Show came to Derby again, and the pavilion was once more erected on Osmaston Hall's Park. This view shows King George V making a visit on that same day. The gentleman in the white waistcoat is Alderman W.G.Wilkins (who had been Mayor in 1912). 125,828 people attended on this occasion. L102

hall at Osmaston, along with its fine parkland by William Emes and gates by Robert Bakewell, to the Fox family, Derby relations of the Strutts. They left in 1888 when the Wilmots – by now called Wilmot-Horton – sold the house and part of the estate to the Midland Railway. They used the house as offices, laid a siding almost to the front door and used the northern part of the park to build the carriage and wagon works. On the part which lay east of London Road a small suburb grew up (Wilmorton, qv.) and houses crept along the Osmaston Road and London Roads. Much later the railway company's successor, the LMS, built the Railway Engineering School to a dignified and convincing neo-classical design by W.H.Hamlyn on another portion of the park in 1937, the year before the Corporation of Derby, having acquired the hall, swept it needlessly

The 1933 Royal Show is pictured here, with the houses lining Osmaston Road (left) and the Pavilion (right). Note the very smart Armstrong-Siddeley saloon, left foreground. The showground later became Ford and Weston's yard. L3584, 4435

The Osmaston estate stretched to over 3,700 acres, and William Emes' parkland was over 100 acres, too. Consequently, when the southern section of the Ring Road was being built c.1930 it was called Osmaston Park Road. This view, in February 1931 shows surfacing taking place, using a steam roller. Beyond – incredibly – the road narrows of the bridge over the LMS Derby-Birmingham main line. L2184

It is April 1934, and Derby's most important new traffic artery, the Ring Road, is still obliged to narrow to barely two lanes to negotiate the railway. This view echoes the previous one, except that the photographer (both were taken by Messrs Hurst and Wallace of Derby) is nearer, and one can see Peartree Station in some detail. Portland Street, left. L2185

away, followed after the war by the church itself and in 1986 by the vicarage.

From 1907 Rolls-Royce built their works on another part of the park, and after 1921 a municipal estate and school grew up around it. In 1929-32 Osmaston Park Road was pushed through the southern edge of the estate and also lined with council housing, although a public park was fashioned from some of what remained with a sports track almost alongside it. The hall site and that part of the park lying between the Osmaston and London Roads was built over for the Ascot Drive Industrial estate and the Municipal Bus Garage from 1948. Ascot Drive lies on the entire course of the two drives which served the house.

Osmaston became mainly part of Derby 1901, the rest was added to Sinfin Moor. In 1904, a new parish was created out of Osmaston. A church, Vicarage and ancillary buildings were designed by the gifted local arts-and-crafts architect Percy Heylin Currey of Little Eaton (1864-1942) for his brother Revd L.S.Currey (1869-1952) first vicar and patron of the badly-needed new church appropriately dedicated to St Osmund which, happily, still flourishes on the London Road, beside the course of the defunct canal.

Further reading:

Craven, M.	*Illustrated History of Derby,* (Breedon 1988) 138-44, 183-84, 215, 226
Craven, M. & Stanley M.	*The Derbyshire Country House* (Breedon, Derby, 1991) 156-58
Holden, W.H.	*The Descent of Humberholme, in Osmaston-by-Derby* in Derbyshire Archaeological Journal LIV (1933) If.
Payne, C.J.	*Derby Churches Old and New* (Derby 1893) 80-88, 210-17

Osmaston Park Road was eventually completed and lined with council housing, the array of neat dwellings breaking on the south side only for roads off and the entrance to Osmaston Park, seen here in an official view of 1935. The park, once Ash Wood and the only surviving part of that in which Osmaston Hall once lay, was opened 8 June 1922 with bowling greens and tennis courts. L4692

A view of 1948 along Osmaston Road. Gone is the Royal Showground – on the right is merely the palisade of Ford and Weston's yard. Note the blackout stripes remaining round the poles supporting the lighting standards and trolley bus wires, and the original pre-war Belisha beacon, left. Astoundingly there is only one road vehicle visible, and children play unconcernedly in the road!

Peartree

Name: Simply, what it says. Applied to a local farm at an unknown date.

PEARTREE Farm lay between Litchurch and New Normanton and by the eighteenth century had come into the possession of the Peach family. William Peach (1760-1843) left it to his son John, his elder son (William) running an ultimately unsuccessful iron foundry on City Road. When John died in 1861, his widow, Ann remained for a while before the whole farm was sold up and some was fairly quickly laid out as streets, the pretty brick and stone farmhouse being demolished. The remaining portion of the farm was sold to the government to make land available for the construction of Normanton Barracks, 1877.

Much of the land near to the Derby to Birmingham railway line (built as the Birmingham and Derby Junction Railway in 1837-39) lay in Litchurch and was purchased by Sir Francis Ley, 1st Bt. (as he became) who erected his Vulcan malleable castings works there in 1874. The works was massively enlarged some years later after Sir Francis went to America and secured the rights to manufacture in the UK of the Ewart Chain Belt. The spin-off from Francis Ley's American journeys was an abiding enthusiasm for baseball. So much so that in 1888 he built a ground near his works and put together a team. By 1890

A view approximately eastwards down the lower part of Malcolm Street in about 1970. The road crossing in the distance is Colombo Street, and beyond, the barrier marks the entrance to Ley's works, with one of its distinctive office buildings behind. The house nearer the camera on the right is a larger-than-average (for the area) double fronted one. Today everything has been swept away. L5590

there was a four-team league and a National Association in 1894. A year later, however, with baseball in decline, the Derby County Football Club had also taken up permanent quarters at the Baseball Ground, where it remains, albeit at time of writing plans are afoot to move Derby County to Pride Park and demolish the football ground to build low-cost housing. The remainder of Leys no longer exists, having been taken over, asset-stripped and demolished in 1986.

Like the West End, Peartree streets were celebrated for their close-knit inter-related communities. Lord Roe's family, as with those of the late Lady Docker (née Royce Turner) and Reg Parnell all hailed from Peartree, and the Shaftesbury Crescent area especially.

The first Anglican church was St Mark, Peartree Road (the latter once the lane connecting Mr Peach's farm with Normanton Road), a mission church of corrugated iron put up in 1879 and replaced by J.Peacock's arresting neo-Norman St Thomas' in 1881. As with other inner city suburbs, these were complemented by numerous dissenting chapels and a complex of schools from 1899. A Carnegie Library was also built to a design by C.B.Sherwin in 1915. Transport invaded the area at the same time as for New Normanton, however.

The demise of Leys has enabled much reconstruction to take place along with new community facilities. Yet most of the terraced housing – much of it not truly uniform terraces, having been built speculatively a few houses at a time – was built late, is of good quality, and survives.

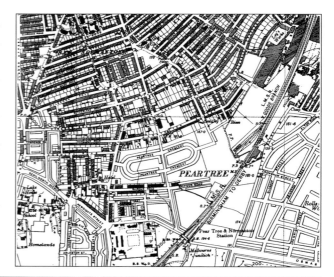

Further reading:
(See also sub. Normanton, New Normanton and Litchurch)

Payne, C.J.   *Derby Churches Old and New* (Derby 1893) 82, 131-36

Quarndon

Name: Old English for 'Mill Hill'

IN Domesday Book Quarndon occurs under the account of Derby (as with Little Chester and Little Eaton) as belonging to the combined College of All Saints and St Alkmund's, the latter having jurisdiction insofar as the church at Quarndon was a chapel of St Alkmund, and it was in the register of the latter that the rites of passage in these three settlements were recorded. The nine bovates of the combined land of Little Eaton and Quarndon yielded the income for the six canons of St Alkmund's.

The chapel of All Saints' (or St Paul) at Quarndon once had Norman fabric, and so must have been erected in the twelfth century; it was under the patronage of the Dean of Lincoln, under whom the Combined College also came from an early date. Richard Cotton acquired it and the estate in 1548 when the college was dissolved, but it was all granted to the Corporation of Derby in 1555 by Mary I to support the incumbencies of St Alkmund's and All Saints, Derby and the Free Grammar School. Much of the land in the village

The old chapel at Quarndon, like the settlement, pertained to the College of St Alkmund and All Saints from the tenth century to the mid-nineteenth century, when it became a vicarage and sundered its ties with Derby. The old church had Norman fabric, but had been thoroughly rebuilt in 1790 shortly before the Revd Joseph Pickford (1772-1844) became perpetual curate of this church and that at Little Eaton in 1803. He was the surviving son of the eminent Derby architect. The church was enlarged in 1835, but mainly dismantled in 1874 when a new church was built nearby. The remains continued in the churchyard as a picturesque ruin, as photographed here by Richard Keene *c.*1889. L8382

belonged to the Mundys of Markeaton and some to the Curzons, who demolished the old hall in 1812. The church was replaced by a new one in 1875 by Giles and Brookhouse ('tasteless and restless' – Pevsner) dedicated to St Paul, there having been some question as to the original dedication. The parish was enclosed in 1808. In the 1840s Dorothy Wilmot-Sitwell purchased some land from Lord Scarsdale (by 1900 the sole landowner) and built a spacious Regency-style villa, later called the Hall and since 1980 the seat of the Bird family, Derby bakers and confectioners. The church became the centre of an independent parish shortly after its building, sundering its ties to Derby and thus technically ending its suburban status.

From at least the eighteenth century there was a sulphur well and mineral water spring, developed by Lord Scarsdale as a Spa. The Gothic well-head still stands, but the flow is supposed to have been curtailed by an earth tremor in 1897.

Since the 1920s a number of modern villas have been erected on land sold in small parcels by the Kedleston estate. One farm, Burley Fields, is all that remains of yet another medieval settlement where a distinctive green-glazed pottery was made in the twelfth and thirteenth centuries – Burley Hill Ware.

Further reading:
Craven, M. & Stanley, M.
The Derbyshire Country House Vol.2
(Matlock 1984) 59
Payne, C.J.
Derby Churches Old and New (Derby 1893)
217-24
Wigley D.A. & Hassall J.T.P.
Quarndon (Derby, n.d. *c*.1965)

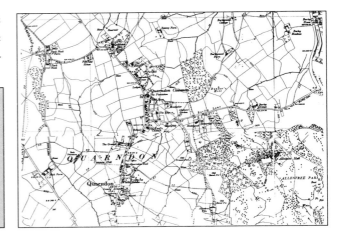

Rowditch

Name: *Rughediche* (1226), Old English, 'Rough Ditch'.

A small enclave astride the Ryknield Street Roman alignment bounded by the Bramble Brook (later GNR line), the Rough Heanor area of Mickleover and California (qv.). It does not appear in the Domesday Book and is first named in a Charter of Burton Abbey, 1226. A settlement mentioned frequently in the Charters of Darley Abbey called Doggelow ('the mound of the dogs') is thought to be synonymous with Rowditch or adjacent to it on the edge of the brook.

Rowditch Farm, an early eighteenth-century house was the property of the distinguished Bateman family, but from *c*.1800 a junior branch of the Harpur family began to exploit the land (west of the Roman Road and south of the brook) for brickmaking, and this industry gradually took over most of the farm, only ending after World War Two.

The focus of Rowditch is really the small settlement centred on the convergence of Uttoxeter Old and New Roads. Yet, on the former, near the line of the railway is Parcel Terrace, laid out in the 1870s on Parcel Fields, so named a being a 'parcel' of land belonging to the settlement. This dramatic night photograph is of a serious fire which destroyed the premises there of Alderman W.G.Wilkins' wallpaper manufacturing firm in 1902. L11109

The west side of Thornhill Farm, looking eastwards across the brickworks towards the factories on Parcel Terrace. Note the railway, left, and newly-constructed Cheviot Street beyond, with the whole of New Zealand rising up behind. Photo from the side of Kingsway taken by Hurst and Wallace about 1933. L3269

The settlement acquired a focus of sorts in 1819 when the newly-turnpiked Uttoxeter New Road diverged from the Old Road (Ryknield Street) eastwards and ran more directly west towards Mickleover. A villa and a small group of houses, an inn and shops grew up around the resulting junction, with small factories on Parcel Fields – perhaps the site of Doggelow – and in 1859 a barracks. In the mid-nineteenth century continual disorder by Parcel Terrace led to it being dubbed 'Little Sodom'!

The barracks closed after barely 30 years however and the buildings converted into a steam laundry. Today, most of these elegant structures survive, but in the ownership of the City Council, which maintains a pleasant park adjacent. The drill square is now tennis courts. The biggest change thereafter was the building of Bemrose School on the site of Elm Tree

Another view of Thornhill Farm, taken on the same occasion as the preceding. This time we can see the front of the farm (now beneath Sainsburys) a bit of railway line beyond and new council housing along Cheviot Street to New Zealand Square, beyond which the thoroughfares have only been pegged out. Right background: Wallace Street, Westleigh Avenue are visible, the left and central background marked by Kingsway. The foreground dump is what then lay at the end of Trowell's Road (now Lane), once the drive to Thornhill, and named after its builder, Col. John Trowell (1744-1825). L2102

Exactly where some of these 'locality' suburbs begin and end is a matter for debate; this view could be deemed to be in Rowditch, California or Littleover. It shows a newly-acquired road roller posed on Manor Road (Rowditch side) looking across to Constable Lane (Littleover side) about 1939. Constable Lane, of course, marks the line of the Ryknield Street, Roman Road, then marked by a hedge line between Manor Road and Rowditch. The chimney is that of the incinerator of the City Hospital, designed by T.H.Thorpe and built in 1931. Edward Saunders, for the same architects, designed the Argosy pub to be built on the grass at left in 1956. O.128

Villa in 1929 and the provision of a dual carriageway on the road west, on either side of which were built municipal houses from c.1930.

It was not until 28 November 1907 that trams ran up Uttoxeter Road (to where the Ring Road would later cross it) being replaced by trolley buses on 13 August 1933, which were extended to the edge of Mickleover at Corden Avenue. The service ceased on 26 November 1966. Much land immediately east of Rowditch was cleared from the 1970s due to an ultimately abortive plan by the County Council to dual the Uttoxeter New Road on the north side, thus destroying many of the best houses of an elegant late Regency and early Victorian suburb. The University took over many of the survivors but have unfortunately demolished three remaining villas, two of Regency date.

Further reading:
Craven, M. *Illustrated History of Derby* (Derby, Breedon, 1988) 29, 37-38, 53, 71, 132, 135, 183, 185, 187-88, 199-201, 221.

Shelton Lock

Name: From a lock on the Derby canal, built 1796 and named after a local family, a member of which probably first kept the lock.

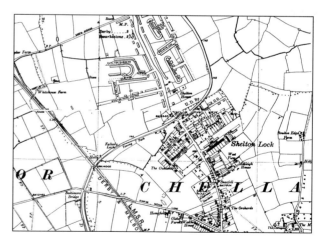

THE Sheltons came from nearby Weston-on-Trent, and George Shelton was manager of Tomlinson and Harpur's brickworks at Chellaston in the 1850s. Shelton Farm was a few yards north of the lock until the 1930s when it was submerged in building. Apart from the Bridge Inn – a canal-inspired hostelry rebuilt in the 1920s – nearly everything at Shelton Lock was built in the decade following.

After World War Two the Derby Rotary Club proposed that a settlement be established as a war memorial and to house disabled ex-servicemen and their families. A target of £100,000 was set and the scheme launched at Shelton Lock in 1947 to be run by a co-operative of 24. The first stage was opened by HRH Princess Elizabeth (HM The Queen) on 27 July 1949 and by 1972, 38 dwellings were occupied.

Some of the housing developed as part of the war memorial village in the 1948-52 period, photographed when new. The scene is Walton Avenue. L4521

HM The Queen as Princess Elizabeth laid the foundation stone for the war memorial village as part of her visit to Derby 27 June 1947. The Mayor was Alderman G.F.Warburton, the last man to serve two terms in that distinguished office. A nice view across what was to become Merrill Way to pre-war Westgreen Avenue is visible behind. L4522, L2165

Today the village is a flourishing integral part of Shelton Lock graced, since 1993, by the statue of a British 'Tommy' erected initially as a World War One memorial outside Allenton British Legion. The suburb was fully integrated into Derby in 1968.

Further reading:
Anon,   *Spotlight on Derby* (Derby, n.d. 1956) 35-37
Swainson, C.M. *Waterways to Derby* (Cromford, 1993) 47, 49.

Sinfin

Name: in 1086 *Sedenefeld,* possibly Old English for 'wide fen (or valley)', but professor Cameron has written (1959) 'A difficult name which must remain an unresolved problem.' The popular 'swine fen' will not do.

I N 1066 Ulfkell held the manorial estate which was one of the few around Derby not to have suffered a disastrous loss of value between that date and the compilation of the Domesday Book: it was 10/- (50p) on both dates probably due to its moorland nature. By the latter date it was held from Henry de Ferrers by William de Rolleston, whose granddaughter brought it in marriage to the Toke family.

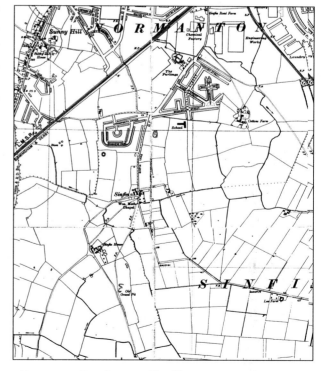

Attached to the hamlet (which never anciently had a church, being part of the parish of Barrow on Trent) was a large area of moorland – Sinfin Moor – of just over 941 acres. 106 acres of this were part of the Derby parish of St Michael, attached to Alvaston, the rest was an extra-parochial liberty split up between the freeholders of Alvaston, Arleston, Sinfin, Barrow, Boulton, Chellaston, Normanton, Osmaston and Swarkestone by an Act of Enclosure of 1802. On it were held, during the

A much changed scene today! Photographed in 1924, this is the centre of the township of Sinfin as it then appeared. Sinfin Lane is ahead, and what is now Redwood Road diverges, left. On the right is the surviving farm, an eighteenth-century building then on the Harpur-Crewe estate, with an earlier core. The building near right, revealed itself to be a largely stone built medieval predecessor to the farm on demolition in 1986; a great loss. L2253

eighteenth century from at least 1733 (and formerly from 1748) the Derby Races, complete with prefabricated grandstand and other portable paraphernalia. The enclosure forced this memorable August festival to re-locate to The Holmes, however.

Parts of Sinfin came into the Borough in 1934, followed by more in 1968, although a good proportion still remains outside the city. From 1968 the part within Derby was swiftly developed into a very large housing estate endowed with largely Scottish names, three inns and a superstore; by 1975 the area contained 6,750 people. Parallel development has also been permitted south of the City boundary by the South Derbyshire District Council. Neither is doing much for the visual and ecological integrity of the Trent Valley hereabouts. The ownership of the land was latterly in the hands of the Harpur-Crewes of Calke Abbey, whose willingness to sell after the 1968 boundary changes made the development (in part financed by the Co-operative movement) possible.

Sinfin Lane began to be built up in the mid-1920s, the first phase of the Austin estate leading the way. In 1928 the new town boundary reached as far south as Cottons Farm (qv) releasing a great deal of land for building. Amongst the earliest developments, even before that, however, were various factories, as here in another 1924 view of Sinfin Lane looking south. At least the road is metalled here!

The County Hotel, Sinfin Lane was opened by Messrs Offiler's brewery in 1934, and is architecturally akin to the Mitre (Allenton) and the Nag's Head, Mickleover, suggesting that the architects were Messrs T.H.Thorpe. L7754

After widening the railway bridge, the bus route was electrified during the war – in August 1943 – and this photograph was taken in the 1950s. The trolley buses were ended on this route on 1 January 1966. Photograph of 1954. L2181

The release of land after 1928 is clear from this view of workers on the way home from one or other of the newly-constructed engineering works south of the railway bridge, seen here. The sign advertises the Sunshine estate, Sinfin Lane, with plots being marketed by Rayboulds. The bus is Derby Corporation no.36, a Guy Invincible, new a year before Hurst & Wallace took the picture in 1931. L2186

Sinfin Lane, looking south, with F.W.Hampshire's works at the far right. Photograph by Hurst and Wallis, 1948. In the distance the houses of the Shakespeare Street estate (qv Cottons) built in the early 1930s.

On the opposite side of Sinfin Lane to the preceding view is Wordsworth Avenue, seen here on the corner of Grasmere Crescent – the exception to the naming scheme being Wordsworth's home rather than another poet! Photograph by Hurst and Wallis, 1948. L11510

Two views taken by Hurst & Wallis in Sinfin Lane, showing the 1930s municipal housing. All the streets in this area were named after English poets or men of letters.

Further reading:

Biggs, J.R.   *Sinfin Songs & Other Poems* (Derby 1932)
Craven, M.   *Illustrated History of Derby,* (Breedon 1988) 11, 98-99, 183, 215, 218, 220-21.
Jenkins, H.A.   *History of Sinfin* in *Notes and Queries* 19.5.1950.

One of the many casualties of what little there ever had been of Old Sinfin was this small chapel built by the Wesleyan Methodist community on Sinfin Moor Lane about 1861. This unpretentious building had long been decaying and out of use when this photograph was taken on 17 July 1981. L1960

Spondon

Name: Unlikely as it may seem, *Spondun* in Old English, translates as 'Hill where shingels for tiling abounds.'

THE manorial estate before 1066 was part of the patrimony of the thegn Stori, and here was a priest and church, and an Anglo-Saxon cross fragment survives in the churchyard to attest to its antiquity. There was also a mill, and it was held (with a portion lying in Mapperley) under Henry de Ferrers. Stori also had very considerable influence in Derby itself before 1066, in which he was followed by Walter d'Eyncourt, but Walter seems not to have acquired Spondon. The Ferrers seem to have held Spondon directly – without a tenant – perhaps a measure of its importance, especially as its church controlled the adjacent chapelries of Chaddesden (qv.) and Stanley.

The White Swan Inn, Moor Street, in 1888. Landlord Peter Coxon, his wife and daughters, Frances and Elizabeth, pose at the door of this venerable hostelry. It was listed merely as the Swan in 1774, and was sold to Offiler's brewery in 1896. Coxon was also blacksmith in succession to his father (another Peter), retiring in 1923. The pub came to him from his uncle Thomas who had married the daughter of the previous landlord, John Bennett. L2958

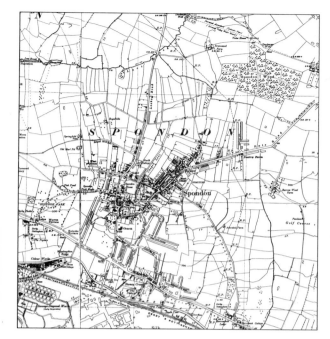

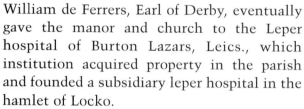

Apart from Locko Park, mercifully lying outside the City boundary, all the important houses in Spondon have gone, with the exception of The Homestead: Spondon Hall was one loss, having been taken over from George, Sir Henry Fowler's second son, in 1941 and turned over to the army. By the war's end it was a wreck and after a decade lying derelict, was demolished and UDC council houses built. Its exceptionally pretty *cottage orne* lodge – closely akin to that at Osmaston – was built when the late eighteenth-century hall was altered in Regency taste for Roger Cox (1774-1843) in around 1816. It stood on the corner of Derby Road and Lodge Lane – the road to the hall. Photograph by H.B.Hurst taken in 1921. L2856

William de Ferrers, Earl of Derby, eventually gave the manor and church to the Leper hospital of Burton Lazars, Leics., which institution acquired property in the parish and founded a subsidiary leper hospital in the hamlet of Locko.

The church, dedicated to the Mercian Saint and Royal Princess, Werburgh (d.699) is notable for being almost entirely of one build, its predecessor having been destroyed (along with much of the village) by fire in Spring 1340-41. In 1826, however, a restoration of questionable scholarship brought about a number of changes which marred the perfection of the whole.

The village has been dominated since the Reformation by those who held the Lordship of Locko: in medieval times and later the Birds (not related to the confectioners), then the Gilberts (kin by marriage to Shakespeare) and subsequently the Lowes and Drury-Lowes. The separate manor held by Burton Lazars was left to the Pipard family and from them came to the Twyfords. The Sallows of Stanton-by-Dale and their heirs the Pilkingtons also had a small estate as did several other local families. Thus the land ownership in more recent times came into the hands of a large number of small freeholders, which made the acquisition of land for development and expansion from the 1870s relatively simple, a process encouraged by the building of the main Nottingham-Derby railway through the parish (with a station) in 1838-39.

Subsequently only the land owned by the Drury-Lowes of Locko remained a barrier

The road from Spondon to Dale Abbey – Dale Road – is seen here *c.*1901. The cottages on the right were built as agricultural labourers' cottages by the Locko estate allegedly in 1820, although the coloured brick banding and stone lintels would suggest that this date is some forty years too early. Only in the years before World War Two did development of the village push further east from this point. The sign on the house (almost extreme right) advertises the services of David Latham, boot maker. L9126

against unsightly development, and even when the parish was absorbed by Derby in 1968, Locko Park itself was not included.

In the 1900s a large paint works (Leech, Neal & Co) – now a notorious scrapyard – was built and in 1916 Courtauld's built a chemical plant on the south side of the railway line, later vastly expanded to produce (as British Celanese) artificial fibres for the garment trade.

Development took place as the Field House estate of the Devas family, the Homestead estate of the Cades, the hall estate of the Cox's and others were sold up between the wars. After the war the hall was demolished and the new A52 'Borrowash by-pass' was built through the park (later infilled with municipal housing) on a concrete causeway of extreme hideousness.

In 1945, Spondon was a delightful hill village with a rich legacy of historic buildings. Yet, over the 30 years following, the built heritage of the village suffered more than most from the ugly effects of civic philistinism. By the time the future city of Derby took over in 1968 much damage had been done, although the trend was not really reversed for another decade.

Around 1916 Courtauld's, later called British Celanese (and now Courtauld's again!), came to Derby to make artificial fibres. This 1933 scene shows part of the workforce heading home across the railway line by Spondon Station on a winter evening. Many of them would be turning right to catch a train into Derby; few would have then lived in what was still the relatively small village of Spondon. The Moon Hotel (background) was completed by Offiler's brewery in 1929 to replace the demolished Station Inn. L8278

Further reading:

Brighouse, G.	*Memories of Spondon* (Derby 1989)
Craven, M. & Stanley, M.	*The Derbyshire Country House*, Vol.2 (Matlock 1984) 33, 66.
Craven, M. & Stanley, M.	*The Derbyshire Country House*, (Breedon, 1991) 129-31
Hughes T.R. & Stevens P.	*Spondon in Old Picture Post Cards* (Zaltbommel, 1994)
Watson, S.	*Spondon, A History* (Derby 1989).
Watson, S. et al.	*Spondon Liberal Club, the First Hundred Years* (Ashbourne, 1992).

Across the Railway from Leech, Neal's works, and adjacent to British Celanese, was built in 1907 the Derby Corporation Sewage Disposal Works, reached via Megaloughton Lane. It was extensively rebuilt and enlarged 1946-61. In this 1948 view two Corporation Sewage Disposal officials walk in through the Megaloughton Lane entrance. L2172

The works undertaken to expand and improve the sewage works at Spondon continued throughout the 1950s. So proud of it all was the council that they issued a postcard, seen here, *c.*1950.

An aerial view taken 21 April 1928 of the paint factory of Leech, Neal & Co. The firm began on Markeaton Lane before 1800 as Benjamin Challinor, William, the son, moving the works to City Road in the 1830s. Around 1870 Alderman Charles Leech (1836-1897) and Thomas Neal took the firm over, expanding to an existing additional works in Spondon (from 1875 a wagon repair works) by about 1890. The site is now Albert Looms' scrapyard. Note the still-functioning Derby Canal on the left of the works and the Derby-London main line on the other side. Raynesway bridge would later be built just out of shot, left. The canal bridge is Megaloughton Bridge. Note the well-marked Spondon ridge-and-furrow. The huts, right, were erected in 1916 by McAlpines to house their workforce (mainly hired in Ireland) to build British Celanese, they were later occupied by firemen and others working at Celanese. L4928

Another aerial view taken in *c.*1935, a little further east. In the background, the increasing sprawl of British Celanese – its first product was aviation dope for the fabric-covered war planes of World War One. It swiftly became apparent that such a plant would require prodigious quantities of energy, so a coal-fired power station was built adjacent in the late 1920s. It lay on the west of a meander of the Derwent (foreground) and by this time a leat had been made cutting off the northerly loop of the river, coming out above the mill at Borrowash. L4926

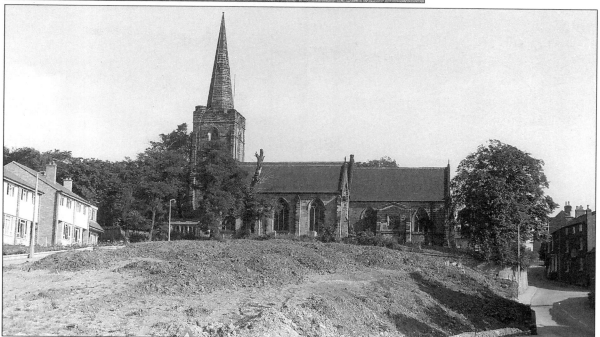

Infill building at Spondon, 1970s. Right foreground, Lodge Lane with Sitwell Street turning off right and Church Lane continuing north. Left foreground, the almost completed houses in Werburgh Close; Gascoyne Drive is going in, foreground. Note a (temporarily) good view of the south side of the church of St Werburgh, entirely built after a serious fire in April 1340, although the spire is half a century later. At the time of the photograph the incumbent was the much-loved rector the late T.E.M. (Tom) Barber (1907-1988) who served the parish 47 years. His magnificent Regency rectory was sold and spoilt as soon as he retired in 1986.

Stenson

Name: *Steintune* in 1086, Old English for 'Steina's farm'.

IN Domesday Book, Twyford and Stenson are entered together, although it rather looks as if Stenson was an outlier of one of the three manors into which Twyford was divided. Most of the land passed to the Tokes from whom it came to the Finderns of Findern whose heiress carried it to the Harpurs of Calke.

In 1796 the Trent and Mersey Canal was built through the parish of Twyford on an alignment approximating to the division between Stenson and its parent village. A later intrusion was the railway line (a spur from the Midland main line from Derby to Birmingham to that from Derby to London). The canal level rises by a lock at Stenson, the

Stenson Bubble, as photographed by Richard Keene around 1890. Incredibly, little has changed. The Trent and Mersey still passes beneath the impossibly narrow bridge with the lock (left) and lock cottages of *c.*1810. In the background Stenson House with its formal two-storey ashlared stone front and vernacular two-and-a-half-storey brick sides still stands four square, as it was built for Harpur-Crewe tenant Richard Forman (b.1793). By 1900 Stenson House was occupied by John Sanders. L8380

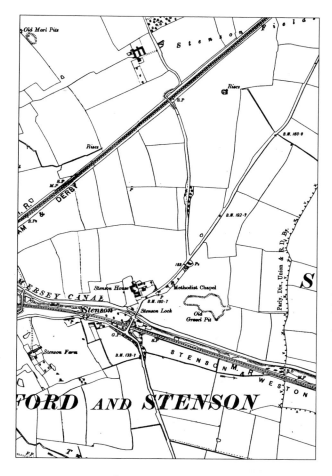

place being called (mysteriously) Stenson Bubble, presided over by Stenson House, a gracious Regency villa built as a farmhouse and model farm for the Harpurs by Samuel Brown of Derby *c*.1815. The farm was sold to the tenants, the Sanders family, by the Harpur-Crewes and the former have developed the farm buildings into an enjoyable inn and the canal bank into a thriving marina. Although not a suburb of Derby in any sense, the nearness of the southern edge of Derby, developed in the 1980s, makes it *de facto* a suburb, especially as boundary revisions and Harpur-Crewe land sales have caused some of the new streets to be built within the township's ancient boundaries.

Strutt's Park

Name: Derives from the ownership, between 1803 and 1861, of St Helen's House and Park by William Strutt FRS (1756-1830) and his elder son Edward, 1st Lord Belper.

THE grounds and park of St Helen's ran from behind Bridge Gate in the south, west of the Derwent, east of Duffield Road (but in the definition used for the creation of the present conservation area and for this description, to include the curtilages to the west) and south of Broadway and Darley Park.

In 1818 William Strutt sold part of the stunning park, laid out in 1767-70 for his predecessor John Gisborne by William Emes of Bowbridge Fields, to Samuel Weatherhead

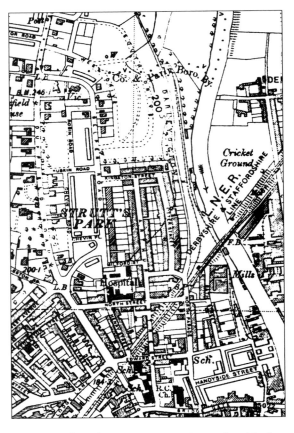

The first parts of William Strutt's Park at St Helen's to be sold was that part between the house and the river. Not only was the Duke Street foundry of Messrs Weatherhead, Glover built there in 1819, but the same year the Bath Street Building Club began collecting subscriptions and erecting cottages. By the 1950s however, their houses had become quite inadequate by modern standards, and the following decade saw them demolished, to be replaced – unsuccessfully in some respects – by Rivermead House (1963), Derby's only domestic tower block. This view of the houses in Bath Street was taken in 1948. L8386

for the erection of an iron foundry, later (from 1848) Handyside's Britannia Foundry, Duke Street. He sold further land to the Bath Street Building Club and to the North Parade Building Club in the year following, and mean artisans' cottages for foundry workers were erected by the former (on River Street as well as Bath Street) and two rather fine neo-Grec terraces of eight houses each were built by the latter on North Parade (formerly a track called Darley Lane) 1819-21 to designs by William Smith.

In 1821 he had also used some land on the east side of Duffield Road to build a very grand villa, Derwent Bank (to a design by his friend Alderman Richard Leaper), in a small park formed out of a hilly part of the existing one. This he sold to Thomas Bridgett, a rich silk throwster, but on Bridgett's death Strutt installed in it his unmarried sisters.

Once St Helen's had sold to Derby School (some years after the initial lease of 1861), much of the parkland was disposed of for re-development, leading to the laying out of Arthur, Edward, North, Margaret and Otter Streets, on which terraced housing was built gradually in the years up to the turn of the century. In 1879 W.H.Worthington, who had bought the Derwent Bank estate, sold all but seven acres for building, and on this Belper Road and Kingston Street were pitched. Derwent Bank was finally sold up and demolished in 1924-25, whereupon Bank View Road and more housing on Duffield Road was built, and the rest of the grounds were turned into a public park which today merges seamlessly into

Once the foundry in Duke Street (from 1848 Messrs Handyside's) had finally ceased to trade, the Borough Council bought the site and laid out Handyside Street and Buchanan Street – the latter named after a notable manager of the Duke Street works. This 1950s view gives a glimpse of this small estate.

From 1879 the part of St Helen's Park further from the house – north of North Street – was sold for development, the streets being laid out with names relating to the Strutts. Otter Street bore the surname of the wife of Edward Strutt, 1st Lord Belper (1801-1880), who was Amelia Harriet, a daughter of William Otter, Bishop of Chichester. The back gardens on the east side hang precipitously above Darley Grove a fact which can be appreciated in this photograph of Derby School Rowing club on the river in the 1930s. L8451

Darley Park. By 1931, Handyside's Duke Street foundry had gone bankrupt for the second and final time and the area was redeveloped with council houses. The railway tracks were eventually ripped up 20 years later (including a head-shunt halfway down leafy Darley Grove) and more housing was built: Derby's only municipal tower block, Rivermead House (1963) and nearby Britannia Flats (1985). A large narrow tapes mill survives, built adjacent by Alderman George Holme (1813-1896) in Bath Street in two stages 1845 and 1868, the latter to a design by S.Mosley. Also surviving is the medieval holy well long dedicated to St Alkmund. Another well, recorded in the cartulary of Darley Abbey and dedicated to St Helen, has long since vanished. Other embellishments to the area survive, too: Joseph Pickford's magnificent St Helen's House of 1767 (Listed Grade 1), W.N.Pugin's important Catholic Church of St Mary nearby (although the Presbytery has been replaced) and 11 Bridge Gate (1730 and later) by William Trimmer.

The whole suburb became a conservation area in 1991, partly to protect Duffield Road, an intact later Victorian suburb, from further 'infill' when some of the larger and earlier villas were sold off by the hard-up County Council, who owned several of them. Yet this essential safeguard was over-ridden in respect of Parkfield (a fine Regency villa extended to make a Maternity Hospital in 1928) within months. It was demolished and the site infilled with some 20 'executive homes' of lamentably pretentious design, thus making a mockery of the whole concept of conservation areas. Two houses

Duffield Road marks the boundary between Strutt's Park and the West End as far as Five Lamps. The road was turnpiked in 1756 and its course moved westwards away from the two country house parks. This is its lower end, south of Five Lamps, looking towards St Helen's House (just visible above the car) and the New Inn (immediately right of All Saints' tower), about 1925. On left, the corner of North Street. L11208

A few yards north of North Street, Kedleston Road diverged to the north-west, a junction which, at the turn of the century, was widened with the pitching of the lower end of Belper Road. To grace the new junction, the four branched, five-lampion standard which had for the previous 61 years graced the conjunction of Cornmarket and Victoria Street, was transplanted, and swiftly gave its name to the area. Yet by 1920 it had been carelessly scrapped to accommodate the motor car, although the name has endured. Photograph *c.*1912 shows, behind the Lamps, The Elms – a house built by the Davenports, silk manufactures *c.*1800 and recently restored as flats, and Park Grange, built *c.*1865 for Charles Bowring to designs by Charles Humphries, now owned by the County Council. L11830

As Duffield Road north of Five Lamps began to become built up in the 1890s, a pavement and retaining walls were put in, for the road itself had sunk since 1756 with use and lack of adequate metalling. This was decorated with a cast-iron balustrade and chain link fence, seen here about 1928. The second house from the right is Austwick, designed by Barry Parker (1867-1947) and Sir Raymond Unwin (1863-1940) for J.T.Robins and recently added to the list of buildings of Historic and Architectural importance, in spite of being harled later in pebbledash. L11852

in this development were indeed purchased by Derby City councillors *abinitio!*

Contrarily, a benefit has been the removal, in the late 1960s, of the 1876-78 Great Northern Railway line which once ran through the park at St Helen's and across Duffield Road in a deep cutting. Nevertheless Strutt's Park remains a compact and still elegant suburb.

Parallel with Duffield Road (from Five Lamps to Burleigh Drive) runs Belper Road, pitched in 1889 on the park of Derwent Bank. It was built up from *c.*1895 to 1935. This view, showing the corner of Ruskin Road, is from the 1920s. L8790

Further reading:
Craven, M.
The Derby Town House (Derby, Breedon, 1987) 89-95, 106-07
Craven, M.
Illustrated History of Derby, (Derby, Breedon, 1988) 11, 183.

The house on the far right at top of previous page was W.A.Reid MP's Allerton Mount, which is clearly from the same architectural hand as the semi-detached pair shown here: Southfield and Northfield. The houses were built *c*.1893-94 for William Gilbert Haslam (1855-1935; Southfield, right) and Edwin Haslam (1843-1913; Northfield, left). William was a director of Haslam's Union Foundry, City Road; Edwin was the gifted continuator of his father's revival of decorative wrought-iron work. By 1908, the former had moved across the road to the far grander North Lees, built by his brother Sir Alfred. Note the Haslam dog in this photograph, taken by a member of the family *c*.1900. Courtesy Mr & Mrs P.Haslam. L 4413

Below: Opposite the Haslam residences lay, until its demolition in 1992, the Queen Mary Maternity Hospital, founded in 1928. The hospital was originally a particularly stylish Regency villa called Parkfield attributable to Alderman Leaper with pilasters at the angles. The capitals and window lintels were decorated with a Greek revival grooved motif which owed a lot to Sir John Soane; inspiration. The house, which retained most of its delightful grounds – embellished with an urn from the parapet of the 1731 Guildhall (where is it now?) was extended and altered with a new entrance (left) in the 1880s by Alderman Sir John ('Brassy') Smith (1828-1897) proprietor of an important brass foundry. Most of the decorative brasswork in the house was made by his craftsmen. The extension of 1928 (right) was no beauty, but was largely invisible from the road. In 1993 the site was destroyed utterly, being replaced by densely-packed detached houses of gimcrack design and poor detailing. The dignified unity of Duffield Road was thus lost and similar developments can hardly be prevented. Photograph of 1947. L11213

Further up Duffield Road, also on the west side, stands The Mount, now called Stanley House. This was erected to the designs of local architect Benjamin Wilson, whose 1851 perspective view, drawn for the client, Thomas Swingler – ironfounder and partner of Eastwood (see Littleover) – is seen here. It was vastly extended in 1882 for Henry Swingler and again in 1976 (to no good aesthetic effect) to make an old peoples' home. Stanley Close now obscures the foreground it leads to other modern houses. Beyond is a small villa of c.1830 by Joseph & Thomas Cooper of Derby – The Knoll – still an unspoilt gem today. L6861

Strictly speaking this view falls almost outside Strutt's Park and into Darley Abbey. It is Duffield Road beyond where today Broadway (pitched 1933-34) joins, from a view of c.1908. The light coloured house, left, then new (now no.183), is two doors up from the Broadway Inn, once an early Victorian villa called Tresilian, lived in by John Peacock. On the latter's garden has appeared no.181. No.183 was home to G.H.Wilson. Beyond, barely visible, is Mile Ash House, then home to Alderman W.H.Marsden, an ex-Mayor and his brood; the taller chimneys are those of 187 (Darley Hill), then occupied by Miss Topham. On the right, in the distance, the little toll cottage (see Darley Abbey). All a great contrast to Bath Street, three quarters of a mile south, where we began the tour of this suburb. L1183

West End

Name: Colloquial, and coined in the nineteenth century. The area is on the west side of Derby.

THE West End owes its origins to the Improvement Act of 1792. This released the surviving part of Nuns' Green – a spacious tract of land transferred from the dissolved Convent of St Mary de Pratis (or Kingsmead) to the Corporation of Derby by Queen Mary I in 1555 – for redevelopment to raise money to pave the streets of Derby and provide adequate street lighting. The Markeaton Brook flows through the area and opponents of the scheme of 1792 were quick to realise that this

The nearest part of West End to the city centre was Willow Row, parallel to which was Goodwin Street, from St Helen's Street to Walker Lane. It was an area of very early housing and tenements, densely packed and classed as a slum from the turn of the century. Clearance began about 1930 with half Goodwin Street, Willow Row, west side of Walker Lane and Wright Street. During this process, recorded in this view of *c.*1931, opportunity was taken to drive a new street called Cathedral Road from the far end of Willow Row to the Walker Lane/Goodwin Street junction, towards which the camera of Messrs Hurst & Wallis is pointing. Note derelict houses of *c.*1800/1810 with their York sashes (left) and grim tenements of mid-Victorian date on Walker Lane (right). Today unnamed Goodwin Street connects Walker Lane with the A52/Ford Street, and Cathedral Road has absorbed the upper (widened) segment of Walker Lane. L5548

Clearance of the properties at the west extremity of Goodwin Street (where they were two-and-a-half-storey buildings of c.1810-20) did not begin until 1956. This view of 25 April 1957 shows the job nearing completion. Still standing – but gutted – are the houses on the east side (note St Alkmund's un-truncated spire behind). The break between the two locks of buildings is Charles Street, which connected to the next parallel road, Orchard Street. Ultimately, all that can be seen here vanished beneath the asphalt of the Inner Ring Road a decade later. L5378

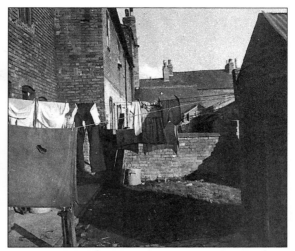

Even on 25 April 1957 some properties in Goodwin Street were still occupied – hence the washing in this view. In the background, the roofs of similar houses in St Helen's Street. L5384

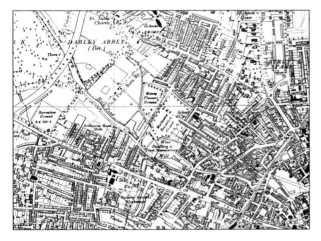

obvious power-source could swiftly lead to the erection of mills and all associated industrial squalour. In contrast to the elegant houses built as a result of the 1768 Nuns' Green Act on Friar Gate, this struck them as a potential calamity.

Nevertheless, with the powerful support of the Strutts, Cromptons and Evanses – the core of Derby's entrepreneurs and bankers – little could be done and William Strutt was appointed chairman of the resulting Improvement Commission with far greater powers at his disposal even than the Corporation. He went on to serve 37 years in this capacity.

Objectors were, however, proved correct, for the brook soon attracted industrialists who indeed erected factories and housing for their workers. Unfortunately, few were philanthropic employers like Strutt, whose workers' housing was built to the highest standards of the time, and most West End housing was extremely substandard, and much of the area soon declined into poverty and degradation.

Nevertheless, the commissioners, and Charles Finney (1773-1828) their architect, laid out new streets to generous standards, including sewers and drainage, and Finney built quite a few of the better houses himself, notably in Bridge Street, a Commissioners' thoroughfare. They also provided in 1828 a fine Gothic Church on that self-same street, St

Agard Street was one of the first to be pitched after the 1792 Improvement Act. This row of houses on the south side of the street were the first to appear after Francis Agard (1730-1816) built his mill on the other side, by the Brook. What looked like four quite substantial and stylish double fronted houses terraced together were actually eight tall artisans' cottages, for each Doric doorcase hid a recessed portico off which led two front doors. This sophisticated row of *c.*1808-10 relates stylistically to the 16 houses of North Parade and this may be by the architect of the latter, William Smith (1784-1851). Local legend declared them to have housed wardens at the County Gaol in Friar Gate, built half a century before, which is perfectly possible. The photograph was taken in 1970, when they were derelict, and about six years prior to their demolition. L10888

John's, designed by Francis Goodwin (1784-1835) a talented London architect who had just completed the County Gaol nearby. Later, in 1872-73, a second church, St Anne's, Whitecross Street, was built to the designs of F.W.Hunt, to cope with the continuing expansion of the suburb.

Strutt himself provided a school in 1812 in Orchard Street (a location which brings home how close to the town centre the West End extended – i.e. to Walker Lane). It was run along the lines advocated by his great friend Joseph Lancaster. Some particularly fine schools were also added to St John's in Mill Street in 1846 to designs by Thomas Cooper (1787-1850). Park land was provided, rather late in the saga of the area, it must

Plenty of the other housing in the West End went back to a period quite soon after the Improvements Act. This view of Little Parker Street shows cottages built very early in the nineteenth century, including what had been an original shop, with fluted pilasters, later converted to a residence, with the stall-riser replaced by later, meatier brickwork. Photograph taken c.1956. L3321

be admitted, on either side of Mackworth Road around the turn of the century, and then only through the philanthropy of Mr and Mrs Mundy of Markeaton Hall, whose land it was. These parks were: Markeaton Recreation Ground (1895), an open-air swimming pool adapted from the brook by damming (1903) and the Mundy Pleasure Ground (1905). Also in the West End was built Derby's first block of flats – Cavendish Buildings, Ford Street, by William Wigginton 1848 (demolished 1924).

Below: Little Parker Street connected Back Parker Street with Parker Street, and is seen here in another view taken at the same time as the preceding. Note the electric delivery van. L3321

Later streets tended to have better houses. After 1859 a committee of the Borough Council was set up to examine building schemes, especially in the light of sanitary arrangements and water supply, the aim being to avoid the building of further potential slum property. This is Cowley Street, looking south towards Mackworth Road, *c.*1970. The street was pitched about 1880 and the houses visible here date from about a decade later, and were a great improvement on those provided by employers in Parker Street or Goodwin Street.

The few houses on Searle Street had been nothing to write home about, and had to vie for space with Alderman Albert Green's Mill. In this view only one (three storey) house survives, right; the remainder by the time the view was taken in 1971 had gone. In the distance is the distinctive roof line of Ryknield Mill, built about 1821 by Thomas Bridgett. Nearer, note that pedestrians passing down Searle Street could cross the Markeaton Brook on a pretty lattice girder bridge, sadly removed because it became unsafe early in 1978. L10887

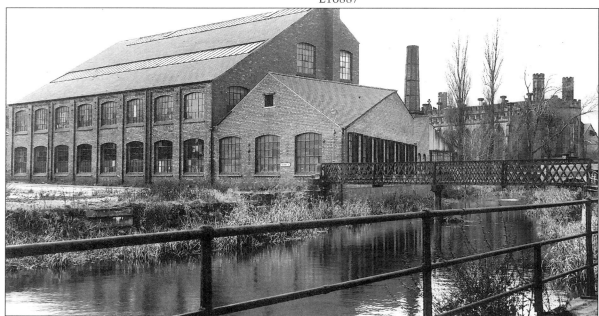

A view of Searle Street footbridge from Brook Walk, *c.*1969. Note Albert Green's mill, with St John's church Bridge Street beyond, long shorn of its ogiform pinnacle caps. A massive development by the University which resulted in yet more student accommodation on the site of Longdon's Mill, Agard Street, actually includes a plan to re-instate this much-loved footbridge. In 1990, the Brook Walk itself was 'facelifted' by the council, which rather sanitised its charm whilst at the same time drawing in various less desirable denizens of the city's byways.

Markeaton Street becomes Markeaton Lane roughly where the ancient Markeaton Mill once stood at the head of its dam. The mill was almost certainly one of the ten mills recorded in Derby in 1086, but was replaced at the turn of the century by Moore and Eadie's new (and very handsome) Britannia tapes mill, seen here in the mid-1960s. The domed two-storey porch was once crowned by a fine statue of Britannia which was removed about 30 years ago to the Leicester factory of Moore & Eddy, Murcott Goode & Co. There is some uncertainty as to its subsequent fate, however. This building is now part of the University of Derby (Department of Fine Art) and there exists an imaginative and grandiose plan to vastly enlarge it. L10874.

Because the West End contained some appalling slums, the plans to clear these were drawn up as early as 1878-79 (Walker Lane – seventeenth and eighteenth-century buildings turned into tenements – and Goodwin Street, very early multi-storey workers' house, qv.) but a start was not made until the 1890s – with Willow Row and Walker Lane. The majority of the West End, where adversity had welded a truly astonishing sense of community and affection in the first half of the twentieth century, was cleared from the mid-1960s (not wholly successfully, much of the replacement housing had itself to be extensively modified two decades later) and remarkably little of the old West End survives today. Somehow, although the new West End is nowadays a far better place (three major University student residences have recently been completed there), it lacks the *esprit de corps* of days gone by.

A view down Lodge Lane and Bridge Street, 20 April 1968. Note the distinctive gable end of the tall portion of Ryknield Mill, left. The West End is in renewal: everything between Garden Street, Green Street and Brook Street has been demolished, and in the distance arise the vastly unpopular maisonette flats which replaced the close-knit West End community's original run-down housing. L5425

Further reading:
Craven, M.
Illustrated History of Derby (Derby, Breedon, 1988) 114, 190-192, 195-97, 212.

Goodhead, E.E.
The West End Story (Matlock 1983)

Goodhead, E.E.
West End Tales (Derby, Breedon, 1986)

A view of Brook Street at an earlier stage of demolition, 1968. A row of houses similar to those pictured, right, was miraculously suffered to remain on Brook Street, near its junction with Ford Street, delightfully restored. It is a measure of their spaciousness that they are each divided into two!

Another view in Brook Street, autumn 1968. The maisonettes are rapidly being completed. Yet, so unsatisfactory were they that the City Council were obliged to completely rebuild them 20 years later as conventional houses. At least the old houses weren't replaced by tower blocks – a fact Derby can heartily congratulate itself for, albeit that it was due more to the town's innate conservatism than its unwillingness to recognise a flawed trend!

Looking across Brook Street (utterly cleared) past Banks' Mill down Bridge Street towards St John's church. To the right, the new maisonettes have begun to rise around Nuns' Street. The tall building, on the horizon, right of centre, is St Christopher's Railway Orphanage, Ashbourne Road, itself demolished some fifteen years after this photograph was taken.

Wilmorton

Name: A contraction of the name of the previous landowner, Revd Sir George Wilmot-Horton, 5th Bt. of Osmaston, coined in 1887 and adopted by the post office in that year. There was also a desire to distinguish the area from Osmaston (qv.) as a whole.

HE 20 or so streets which make up this small suburb are (and in some cases, were) all concentrated between Deadman's Lane (an ancient way leading to a former plague pit dug outside the Borough boundary in 1348 during the Black Death) and the Canal Bridge along the east side of London Road.

A view southwards down London Road, virtually from one end (Deadman's Lane, left) to the other (Canal Bridge, in far distance) of the small settlement. Since this 1954 view was taken, the area, left, behind the wall has been developed as the Railway Technical Centre. Behind the Woodbines advert (not then politically incorrect!) is the stylish Portland Hotel (603 London Road) built at the turn of the century and in the 1920s the favourite watering hole of Rt. Hon. Jimmy Thomas, PC, MP (1874-1949) one of Derby's two MPs, sitting as a Labour member 1910-31 and National Labour 1931-36. L11856

This was part of the estate of Osmaston Hall released by sale in the 1880s and built up largely by the Midland Railway for its carriage, wagon and locomotive building workforce. It elected a School Board in 1892, which built a new school (miraculously, still operating) eighteen months later, and the Curreys built the community a very fine church in 1904 (qv. Osmaston). There probably always had been an inn, at least since the canal was built in 1796, The Navigation, London Road, having been in business by 1846, and its owners responded to the new community by rebuilding it to a design by James Wright in 1895. At the same time a very stylish neo-Baroque pub called the Portland Hotel was also built on the corner of Dickinson Street and London Road. The Street names are an eclectic combination of public schools, places served by the Railway and Midland Railway directors.

In 1937 the London Midland and Scottish (as the Railway had become from 1923) erected their almost Nordically neo-classical Railway Engineering School at Wilmorton.

However, immediately south of the residential area and between the London Road and the canal, the County Borough Council formed a refuse disposal site. This later became the place chosen for the building of Wilmorton College of Further Education from the

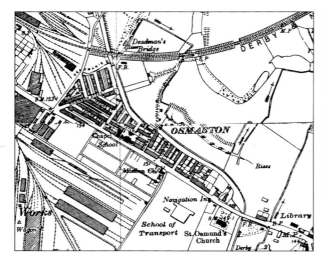

London Road, Wilmorton, near Harrow Street. Much of what can be seen here was cleared in the 1960s to make room for the roundabout which today give access to Wilmorton College, itself built on the former Derby Borough Refuse Tip. What with that and a plague pit at the end of Deadman's Lane (hence the name) underlying a vast gasworks, it might not commend itself as an area to a stranger. Yet it was always a close-knit and friendly community, self-sufficient with its school and church. Photograph taken *c.*1962. L7836

1960s which led to the closure and clearance of one or two streets. Future plans include a major new road from the roundabout where Ascot Drive joins London Road into the old railway works area, now Derby's City

Virtually the north-facing counterpart to the previous view and taken on the same occasion. Note the K3 telephone box beside the Portland (right). L11855

Challenge Site, called (without trace of irony) Pride Park. This is being hotly contested by the residents who sense it would destroy the unique ambience of this very small but distinctive community.

Further reading:

Craven, M.   *Illustrated History of Derby* (Derby, Breedon, 1988) 183-84, 186, 187, 225.

Hodgkin, A. in   *Derby Express* (23/3/1995) p.22 cc1-8.